OWN it

OWN it

Leaving Behind a Borrowed Faith

Michael & Hayley DiMarco

B&H
PUBLISHING GROUP

NASHVILLE, TENNESSEE

978-1-4336-8202-5

Published by B&H Publishing Group,
Nashville, Tennessee

Dewey Decimal Classification: 234.2
Subject Heading: FAITH \ SPIRITUAL LIFE \ SELF

1 2 3 4 5 6 7 8 • 17 16 15 14 13

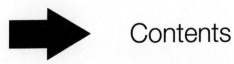

Contents

Disowned

There's an ancient story told of a young man who disowned his father. He cut all ties and just walked away. He
was tired of living at home under his rule. He wanted a
fresh start and independence. He was done being the son
and wanted to be the man, so he told his father to give him
what was rightfully his, but his inheritance wasn't techni-
cally his until his father was dead. In this request for an
early cash-out, the young man essentially told his father he
wished he were dead.

This is the famous story of the prodigal son, told by
Jesus to the men who sat at His feet. In this parable, Jesus
gave the backstory of a boy who wanted to define his own
life, to own his own decisions, and to make his own way,

1

but not without the financing of his father. And so he took from his dad what he needed, to do what he wanted, and he left. He made his way into the life he believed to be far better than living as one controlled and indebted to his father. And he lived relatively free until, ironically, all he had taken from his father had dried up. When the money was gone, so was his joy, his freedom, and his hope. And so after spending time watching pigs eat better than he was, he returned home. Hat in hand and much wiser for the experiences he had lived, he returned with the idea of rejecting his self-serving ways and, instead, fessing up to his royal idiocy and accepting whatever scraps his father would throw his way.

As the child who had previously disowned his father returned, the father was waiting, not with an angry fist or a long lecture, but with outstretched arms. The father proved himself to be worth much more than the inheritance his child had blown; he had never disowned his son even though his son had disowned him. This action alone was worthy of the honor of being called father. Rather than demanding payment from the son for his hurtful and selfish choices, the father gave even more to the son from what he had left.

This story, though put into our own words, came from the mouth of Jesus and it shows how eager God is to lovingly restore those who have wandered. If you have doubts, if your faith is weak, even if you disowned your faith or have been disowned by those who used to love you, this book isn't about accusing you but setting you free. It isn't about rejecting you but helping you to sort it all out. If your faith hasn't disappeared completely from your life but has lost its fire or never has been much to write home about in the first place, this book is for you as well. The difficulty of faith doesn't come from the lack of feeling or even action but from the lack of divine knowledge—the knowledge of who God is and of the depth of His love. Your faith isn't so much about what you have done or not done, but what God has done and how much He has loved you. The most awful thing about faltering faith isn't the human relationships that can suffer, though they are tragedies, but it is the fact that you are missing out on the love and acceptance that God has waiting for you.

When you own your faith, you possess all of the love that God has for you. It covers you, fills you, fulfills you. It takes all the struggles that used to plague you and leaves you with peace. It takes all the sadness and replaces it with joy. When you own your faith, you are a changed human being. You are a safe human being. You don't rely on others to affirm you or to accept you, but you are still able to accept and love them. You are able to love unconditionally and any rejection others may offer is no longer something you take personally. That's because when you own your faith, the love of God eclipses all other loves and, since His love is perfect, solid, and unshakable, you never have to fear again. You are never alone again, never helpless or hopeless.

If your faith has never given you such wonderful things, then have no fear—things can change, but you must be willing to thoughtfully consider the words you will be reading in this book and ask yourself if your understanding of who God is has been accurate or only a shadow of who He truly is. Our goal here is to help you to be free from the doubt that plagues you, the distance that separates you, the weaknesses that cripple you, and the powerlessness that affects you. You may even know it in your head, but do you really own it? At the very least, join us in a conversation about what it means to own your faith and if it's even worth owning. It's our prayer not that you will be indoctrinated but illuminated. Because a life lived in the light is a life that is truly owned by its occupant. So let's discover and uncover what Own It really means.

What Is "Owning" Your Faith?

Weak faith in a strong object is infinitely better
than strong faith in a weak object.
—Tim Keller

Ownership is a powerful thing. It makes people feel things—things like love, pride, responsibility, and even jealousy. Ownership colors a person's view of the object of their possession and its value. What you feel for something you own is completely different from how you feel about something that isn't yours. That's why people tend to care about their own stuff. Ownership feeds devotion and it often dictates action. For example, people tend to take better care of

5

stuff that they own than stuff that they rent. And they love the stuff they own more than the stuff they borrow. How many times have you lent something to someone who didn't take care of it the way you do? When you borrow something, your attention to it is temporary. Ownership conveys permanence. The stuff you own matters to you.

But ownership doesn't just apply to things; it also applies to lives. Have you ever met an animal person who loved their pet so much that they treated it like a child? There are some powerful emotions that come from having a living thing that belongs to you. When people fight for their country, when they fight for their loved ones, it's because they are *their* loved ones. Aren't the other countries and families just as valuable? Yes, but they are not theirs and so they fight for what is theirs. Children, even those who are abused by their parents, are born with an innate ability to love their parents, simply because they are theirs, regardless of how horribly they treat them. Though that can dissipate with time (and abuse), it's there to begin with. And the same is true for parents; they feel a deep sense of ownership for their kids, not the kind of ownership of slave and master, as some kids might believe, but a kind of ownership that instills an enormous degree of love and pride that only your own kids can illicit, no matter how much they may or may not deserve it.

Yes, *when something is yours it becomes immediately more important to you than something that is not yours.* But not all ownership has to do with the legal right to control or do whatever you want with what you own. No, ownership can also apply to a state of heart, a way of living whereby you make what you say and what you do agree. As in when you own your actions, rather than faking your way through life, living a double life, pretending to be something that you aren't in order to please those you love. This double-mindedness becomes evident in matters of faith where it can be easy to hide your true feelings and thoughts, and to put on a good face when all the while you are a confused mess on the inside. And in your uncertainty, an inability to own your faith can result in choices that hurt not only yourself but also your relationships. In this condition, you own neither your beliefs nor your actions, but instead you end up in a no-man's-land that breeds animosity for the very things in your life that you say you love.

In the life of faith, then, *there are conditions of the heart that mimic faith, but are far from a true faith that not only saves, but encourages, repairs, heals, and changes you from the inside out.* These conditions that do not involve owning your faith are founded in the attempt to fake it, borrow it, rent it, or pick and choose it, and ultimately their end is the ultimate act of disowning it.

7

Fake It

When you are faking it you can fool just about everyone. And that's really the goal in faking it; it's to fool those who love you, especially those who want only what's best for you and is certain that being a good Christian *is* what's best for you. When you fake it you do all, or at least most, of the right things; you probably even say almost all of the right things. And everyone looks at you and smiles at the person you are pretending to be, and deep inside you feel rejected. You feel rejected because they love who they want you to be, not who you *really* are. **When you are faking something for the approval of others, even the approval you get is painful because it's based on a lie, and the real you never truly finds acceptance.**

For centuries people the world over have faked their faith, many without even being aware of the fact. They have faked it so well that they even deceived themselves, believing that their actions of faith somehow made up for their disbelief, doubt, and fear. They have walked through life unchanged, numb to the things of the Spirit, and trying desperately to make up for it through determination to be good and obedient. They try to do all the right things, say all the right things, and be just who they believe they should be. Yet all the while they are unable to trust their lives and the lives of those they love to the God who saves.

➡ **Hayley Faked It:** For all of my life I called myself a Christian, even long before I truly was one. I believed in God; I trusted that Jesus was who He said He was. But I lived with fear and doubt. Believing that God was powerful and holy came easy to me, but believing that I was good enough for Him to love didn't. So while I said I was a Christian, *I believed I was a Christian going to hell,* and so I figured since I was going to hell I might as well have fun on the way. And so I gave into my desires; I did stupid stuff—I went too far and I confirmed to myself that my faith was indeed fake. When I saw how badly I was faking it, the guilt consumed me. In turn, guilt just fed my fear and doubt, and the cycle started all over again. Fake faith is tortured and pointless faith. ⬅

When you fake it, you pretend to be, feel, or think something that isn't true, and this dissonance hurts. In the end, faking it results in either fatigue and rejection or a lifelong faking that gives you a faith grounded in deception. How ironic, since **faith is belief in the truth, while deception is pretend belief in something considered a lie.** Deception never breeds truth. So if you, like Hayley, have felt that you've been faking it, in any part of your life—but especially in your relationship to God—then read on as we talk about what it means to own your faith or to be honest about disowning it, rather than just faking it.

Borrow It

When your faith isn't your own, but one that you inherited or borrowed from another, the emotional and spiritual strain that it can put on you *and* the ones you got your faith from can be enormous. Borrowed faith is a cheap imitation of ownership. And that's why it brings so much emotional strain on your life. **When your faith truly belongs to someone else, when you took it out of obligation or even devotion to your loved one, it makes the person you got it from the god of your life.** In them you look for the law that you must follow to be accepted by them; in them you look for your salvation.

If you haven't discovered it yet, your faith in man will ultimately disappoint because the creation cannot handle the worship due the Creator. You see this in the resentment that develops as you fail to be all that your loved one wanted you to be or do all they believe you should do. **When you get your power to be "good" from your desire to please man, you will ultimately fail because you do not have the power to be perfect,** and they do not have the power to give you perfection. That is why your faith lacks passion and power, because that power and passion comes from the Creator and not the creation. When your faith is borrowed, it does not truly belong to you, and because of that, your love and devotion will never ring true. Your words and even actions will never align with your feelings because you have taken what was never yours to begin with and tried to build your life on it. This is a shaky foundation and not the same as owning your faith.

Even if you've borrowed your faith, claiming your salvation comes from the roots of your family tree and believing being "born Christian" is your get-out-of-jail-free card, you are deceiving yourself. The Bible, which defines the Christian faith, says that faith isn't about heredity, but relationship. We know this because of words like these found in the book of Romans: "If you confess with your mouth that Jesus is Lord and believe in your heart that God raised him from the dead, you will be saved. For with the heart one believes and is justified, and with the mouth one confesses and is saved" (Rom. 10:9–10 ESV). It's all about you and not your family or the fact that you were baptized as a baby. **When you own your faith, it starts with your confession and not the confession of those who love you.**

➡ **My Boring Christian Life:** A lot of kids raised in Christian homes complain about the fact that they don't have an amazing testimony like the people who were raised without faith but through some incredibly horrible situations found Jesus and now have amazing testimonies. Some bemoan their peaceful and uneventful lives and wish they could share an Oprah-worthy testimony about what God has done in their life. But alas, life has been pretty picture-perfect and God hasn't really had to show Himself much, so no big stories exist. When that's the case, it can be easy to feel like your faith isn't so compelling and that you don't have much to offer in the way of a story that would draw others into faith. And so you live a spiritually quiet life, not stepping out and proclaiming the amazing power of faith— not risking to question others' beliefs or to offer them a lifeline in yours because after all, you reason, you don't have an amazing story to share. If that sounds like you, then you may have less to worry about than you may think. You see, **you don't have to give up the hope of a compelling testimony, because what compels the nonbeliever isn't your testimony about yourself, but about Him.** If you say you still have no testimony about Him, then your faith may be weakened by the fact that you haven't made it your own yet. But making it your own isn't as hard as going back in time and having a different life story, so there is hope. ←

Now if you say that you are content with a borrowed faith, don't shut the book and walk away just yet—there is something here for you; just give it a chance. You've opened these pages for a reason. Allow God to show you what it is, just this once; allow Him to take you somewhere you never thought you wanted to go and see if He doesn't come through for you. Borrowed faith is simply faith in the wrong thing. And that's why it isn't the kind of faith that changes your life. It isn't the kind of faith that overcomes adversity or changes the world, but when you own it, when you stop mooching and start possessing, the world inside you and around you changes dramatically.

Rent It

When you rent something, you make monthly payments, whereby you keep something and use it for yourself up until the time when you stop making payments. And at that time your use of the thing ends with your payments. You might make monthly or even yearly or weekly payments on your faith, going to church in order to feel

Christian. You might talk about God, pray to God, read about God, and serve God, but if all of that is part of your "payment" for faith, then you're a renter, not an owner. An owner doesn't have to make payments—their faith is theirs by virtue of who *He* is, not who *they* are or what *they* do or don't do.

It can be easy to confuse the life of faith with the act of doing, but they aren't the same thing. Certainly, when you experience God's love and His saving grace, you want to do things for Him and with Him, but it is out of love and not out of necessity as payment for your faith. That price was already paid, and not by you or any other human being, but by God Himself. As it says in Ephesians, "For by grace you have been saved through faith. And this is not your own doing; it is the gift of God, not a result of works, so that no one may boast" (2:8–9 ESV).

The trouble with renting your faith is that it puts all of the reliance for salvation on self-effort rather than on God. When that happens you wear out quickly; you feel burnt out and tire easily of the hard work of obedience, which you believe leads to your salvation. This is what happens when you see a hard-working religious person who has walked away from their professed faith. They put all of their hope in their *ability* to be good, rather than in God Himself. When they run out of strength, they run out of their payment for the faith and end up losing their rental. But when you own it—really own it—you have no need to make payments in order to keep it because it already belongs to you. This is called justification. **You don't have to justify yourself by working hard to gain God's approval.** Just look at the life of Abraham, the father of the faith: "For if Abraham was justified by works, he has something to boast about, but not before God. For what does the Scripture say? 'Abraham believed God, and it was counted to him as righteousness'" (Rom. 4:2–3 ESV). Abraham was righteous because of his undying faith and trust in God. He believed God more than he even believed his own feelings. When God asked him to sacrifice his most prized possession, his son, he believed God was good and so were His commands. Abraham acted, and this undying devotion to God displayed his faithfulness. He was justified by his faith in God, by the Father's ability to be good far beyond Abraham's understanding.

As long as your idea of faith requires you to make payments in order to receive the love of God, you are not an owner but a renter. God doesn't want your payments; He doesn't need them. All He wants is for you to accept *His* payment, the one and only payment ever needed. The payment for your life was His Son's life. And to say that additional monthly checks must be cut to save you is

to say that His Son's death was a waste of a perfectly good life. Rather than endear you to God, this way of thinking cuts you off from Him, as you take His most valuable gift and hand it back to Him in rejection of its value and necessity in your life. Such arrogance then, makes you the only salvation acceptable, makes you your own Messiah, your own perfect lamb worthy of the name Savior.

Pick and Choose It

But maybe you aren't renting; maybe you're just accepting—freely accepting the gifts of God. Maybe you accept His sacrifice with arms wide open. You appreciate all He's done for you and in return you claim Him as your Savior, but you aren't sure about all this Bible stuff. "I mean, how can it all possibly be true, let alone applicable in today's day and age?" So you pick and choose. You are a smart person with intuition, education, and common sense. And you like the way Jesus lived. What He said made sense, for the most part, but some of it had to be hyperbole; some of it was just stories and not meant to be law or anything. Like when He said, "If someone slaps you on the right cheek, give them the other one" (see Matt. 5:39; Luke 6:29)—now that's nonsense. Common sense says you've got to protect yourself. Stand up for your rights. So not everything in the Bible is meant for today, you reason. So being as smart as you are, you've decided to pick and choose. You've read some of it, and you've taken the parts that make sense and made them your own, and the rest? Well . . . out of sight, out of mind. Dealing with it, understanding it, is all too much work and not really necessary. Plenty of people live with only a portion of the Bible as their rulebook. The stuff they like that seems beneficial to them they take, and the rest they claim to be out of date or creative license. This happens a lot in classes that study the Bible as literature and in coffeehouses where the validity of Christ's words and ideas are analyzed and lined up in a cost/benefit chart meant to be used to develop your own kind of theology.

When you practice this kind of picking and choosing, it's like making your own Frankenstein faith. Like the mad doctor who created the monster in Mary Shelley's famous book, you create your own pieced-together religion specially designed to meet your specific needs. As if your editing prowess far outweighs that of the early church fathers of our faith. In this picking and choosing of your faith, what you end up with is as volatile as Dr. Frankenstein's monster and just as ugly, because in your human nature you pick those things that ultimately serve you. Sure, you might subscribe to the need to help orphans and widows, you might see God's call to feed the hungry and care for the weak to be a selfish law to adopt, but when you picked it for yourself, you picked it because of the ultimate benefit it gives you. In other words, it makes you feel like a good person—like you are making a difference, like you aren't a hypocrite, like you are spiritually informed and making decisions that will benefit you in the area of self-esteem as well as salvation. That's because of the reasons you base your picking and choosing on. **When you design your own faith, you must have a criteria for your choices, a line you draw that builds the parameters of your faith, and in this kind of self-designed faith, your human nature designs your beliefs around you rather than God, and in so doing, you subconsciously make yourself your own God.**

Now, anyone with a rudimentary understanding of the concept of God must agree that by definition God is not a being that needs to be saved. If He needed to be saved, then there would need to be someone more powerful than Him to save Him, and then He would not be God but His savior would be. If God by definition is all-powerful, all-knowing, and perfect—i.e., GOD—then **when you make yourself the designer of your own salvation, you ultimately make yourself the all-knowing and all-powerful one in your life.** That means that you are making yourself the god in your life so that you can save yourself, but if you are God, then you don't need saving.

When you pick and you choose your faith, what you are owning is your own inerrancy, or inability to be wrong. You are claiming your perfection and wisdom and rejecting anything that speaks of your failure to be perfect. Unfortunately, when circumstances show you that maybe your chosen path of salvation is too restrictive or getting in the way of your ultimate enjoyment, you are faced with some heavy editorial work. And in those changes to the Scriptures of your faith you only prove that you didn't know what you were doing in the first place. Picking and choosing your faith promises the ultimate freedom to be who you want and do what you want, but eventually it will only prove to you that to live for yourself and to make your law based on your own happiness is to become the slave of your imperfect self and to be tortured and tormented by your own pride and failure.

➡ **Michael's Picky and Choosy Faith:** All of my life I wanted to be married. It was my number one goal in life. I was a Christian and so I knew I would only ever have sex with my wife, but who I defined as my wife was my own choosing. See, when I dated someone I really liked, I told myself I was going to marry her and so I could of course sleep with her. I chose to believe as long as I was going to get married to her, I could have her. And so I thought . . . until I would break up with her. Then the next one would come along and I would tell myself the same thing. In picking and choosing which parts of Scripture I liked and how they applied to my life, I made one mess after another, leaving broken hearts in my wake. And my heart didn't fare so well either. When I did ultimately marry one of the girls, it ended in divorce two years later because I failed to establish my life on the complete counsel of God. Instead, I counseled myself, made up what I thought Scripture should say, all the while calling myself a Christian. I lived as a non-Christian for years. But God will let you wreck yourself in order to save you, and that's what He did for me when I surrendered my whole life and will in a tiny jail cell. My life (and peace) have never been the same all because I've stopped picking and choosing and embraced owning my faith. ◄

Disown It

Who are you? Are you the owner of your faith; are you just faking it, or picking and choosing it; or have you just thrown your hands up and walked away? **When someone disowns an idea or even a person, they give up faith in or love for something or someone they used to call their own.** They look at that idea or person as a royal mistake, and they most often replace it with something or someone else, even if it's just self. Either way, they reject their former belief and so disown, or give up the right to, what they used to have full access to.

When you disown your faith, you turn your back on it and that can leave you feeling all kinds of junk—resentment for the lies you used to believe, distrust or disgust of those who still believe them, fear that you may be wrong, anger for being wrong for so long before. It can be a mix of any of these emotions or one compelling one, but either way, walking away from your faith isn't easy. And in a lot of instances, the pain can come from those you left behind. Because that's just how they feel—rejected along with God Himself—their resentment and anger can build. Their fear over your eternal destination can also cloud their emotions and leave them thinking all kinds of thoughts that only affirm your rejection of their faith in their so-called God of amazing grace. How can they preach His grace and offer you none? How can they speak of His love and forgiveness without sharing in it? And who do they think they are in their wrath and judgment . . . the

Savior? Their inability to know how to handle dissension can only make matters worse, but that's why this book has found its way to your hands, to remove the human ability to make others' decisions personal and to remove demands that not even God Himself makes.

When Jesus was face-to-face with people who disowned Him, argument was not His response. He didn't pursue them, explain the errors of their ways to them; He allowed them to be whomever they were made to be and to make the decisions they would make. There is a story often told of His encounter with a very rich young man who wanted to follow Him. He believed in God. He lived an obedient life, trying hard to do all that God and the Scriptures asked, but when he asked Jesus what more he could do, the answer he got froze him in his tracks: "And Jesus, looking at him, loved him, and said to him, 'You lack one thing: go, sell all that you have and give to the poor, and you will have treasure in heaven; and come, follow me.' Disheartened by the saying, he went away sorrowful, for he had great possessions" (Mark 10:21–22 ESV). But the story doesn't end there. The most intriguing part of this exchange isn't that the man left when he realized God wanted him to give up his obsession for stuff, but that Jesus didn't run after him. He didn't grab his arm and try to explain Himself better. He wasn't worried or upset that the young man wasn't getting it. Jesus allowed the man to do what he would, free from the pressure of His presence.

God does the same today. He doesn't force faith. Even though His followers wish He would, He isn't in the habit of high-pressured sales. Though He is sovereign and nothing happens except that He allows it, He also doesn't force ownership. His hand isn't on the back of your neck forcing you to your knees. As you well know, you can reject Him, disown Him, and walk away from Him and you won't be struck by lightning. He never said you would. He never said that rejecting Him was an impossibility, or instantly punishable by plague or death. If that were the case, then the men who hung Jesus on the cross would have been zapped. But God allows and even uses the rejection of Himself by men to His glory. After all, the cross—the focus of all of God's Word, from beginning to end—was made possible by the very men who believed they were thwarting the work of Jesus. But even their rejection of Him was not only allowed but meant to be. You might think that you have hardened your heart, but the truth is that God is the one who chooses whom He will save and who will reject Him. So even the freedom that you feel, the doubt you have, would not be yours if He had not allowed it. As it says in Romans 9:18,

"He has mercy on whomever he wills, and he hardens whomever he wills" (ESV).

Own It

So, why a book on owning your faith if it is God who ultimately decides the fate of your heart? Why would we even bring up the subject of salvation, of faith, of belief and doubt if we were only pawns in God's game of life? Those questions are valid and are ones that have sparked centuries of debate, argument, and even wars.

Should we spend time talking to you about your doubts, cajoling you, disowning you, fighting for you, or should we just let God do with you what He would do? You've probably already guessed our answer because you're holding a book we wrote on the subject. But to make it clear—"yes," we should spend time helping you with the doubts that plague so many when it comes to faith in the unseen, and "no," we should not and will not cajole, disown, or fight you to faith. As the story of the prodigal made clear, God is a not a God who strikes the doubter dead. He is not a God who forever rejects those who reject Him, but He is a God whose love and power, goodness and kindness is enough to outlove even the most terrible of cynics who wants to believe.

Romans 5:8 tells us that Christ died for sinners, so your doubt does not exclude you from ownership. You may doubt God's love or even His existence, and you might think that excludes you from faith, but doubt isn't as foreign a concept to faith as some would have you believe. Each one of us doubts: we doubt that God can heal our wounds; we doubt that He would really ever let us move a mountain; we doubt that we can overcome our addictions and obsessions even though His Word promises it all. Doubt is a part of the human condition, natural to the state of man who, like an ant trying to figure out the inner workings of a nuclear power plant, is incapable of understanding even the most rudimentary of descriptions of such a powerful entity.

Your doubt doesn't exclude you from faith, no matter what you may have heard—it simply proves your humanness and His unfathomable Godness. But doubt doesn't have to define you or rule you; rather, it can be the fuel for discussion, study, and prayer. In order to own your faith, you have to continue the conversation. You have to allow yourself to be wrong, to question and to be taught. As long as you remain unteachable, rigid in your disbelief and doubt, you will remain in limbo, unable to firmly stand on either your conviction or suspicion. But in either case, to own one or the other you must ultimately be owned by your belief. You are owned by your faith or doubt when you turn yourself over to it fully.

When you are fully owned by your disbelief, then there is no further discussion that needs to be had between you and the God you once trusted. In fact, your very senses are numb to His presence, your eyes shut, your ears closed, and your body turned away. In this instance you have come to grips with the fact that, if need be, you would stand up in front of the world and say, "I deny Jesus is Lord," and you would be content with that denial. But before you jump to your feet, first consider that this verbal rejection of Jesus comes with an effect, and that is that as you deny Him, so He denies you. As He said in the book of Matthew, "Whoever denies me before men, I also will deny before my Father who is in heaven" (Matt. 10:33 esv). So is it any wonder that in your denial of the One who was sent to save you, you have found more and more animosity toward God and His people? That your heart has hardened more with each passing day? This is the result of Jesus denying you more than it is of you denying Him. The truth is that **you own your faith when and only when Christ owns you.** William Barley, in *The Letters of James and Peter,* spoke this better than we ever could when he said,

It frequently happens that the value of a thing lies in the fact that someone has possessed it. A very ordinary thing acquires a new value if it has been possessed by some famous person. In any museum we will find quite ordinary things—clothes, a walking-stick, a pen, pieces of furniture—which are only of value because they were possessed and used by some great person. It is the ownership which gives them worth. It is so with the Christian. The Christian may be a very ordinary person, but he acquires a new value and dignity and greatness because he belongs to God. The greatness of the Christian lies in the fact that he is God's.

To be owned by God is ultimately to be consumed by Him. When God owns you, your mind returns continually to His presence. You can't quit Him. You can't reject Him because He has ahold of you. Many Christian parents claim this to be the case in the lives of their prodigal children. They claim the faith that they were raised in is the seed that will one day sprout and bring them back. And that is often the case. In these situations, the prodigal cannot stop thinking "what if"; they can't get Jesus' face out of their minds and the stain of guilt off of their lives. This is because they are owned, and that ownership has its cost.

The idea of the seeds of faith first got their start in a story told by Jesus in the parable of the sower. He explained faith this way:

"Consider the sower who went out to sow. As he was sowing,

some seed fell along the path, and the birds came and ate them up.

Others **fell on rocky ground,** where there wasn't much soil, and they sprang up quickly since the soil wasn't deep. But when the sun came up they were scorched, and since they had no root, they withered.

Others **fell among thorns,** and the thorns came up and choked them.

Still **others fell on good ground and produced a crop:** some 100, some 60, and some 30 times what was sown. Anyone who has ears should listen!" (Matt. 13:3–9)

This parable was used to help the agrarian listeners of Jesus' time better understand the reasons why faith takes hold in some people's lives but not in others. And to explain what all this meant, He followed up His parable with these words:

> "When anyone hears the word about the kingdom and doesn't understand it, the evil one comes and snatches away what was sown in his heart. This is the one **sown along the path.**
>
> And the one **sown on rocky ground**—this is one who hears the word and immediately receives it with joy. Yet he has no root in himself, but is short-lived. When pressure or persecution comes because of the word, immediately he stumbles.
>
> Now the one **sown among the thorns**—this is one who hears the word, but the worries of this age and the seduction of wealth choke the word, and it becomes unfruitful.
>
> But the one **sown on the good ground**—this is one who hears and understands the word, who does bear fruit and yields: some 100, some 60, some 30 times what was sown." (Matt. 13:19–23)

So let's take a closer look. The one *sown on the path* clearly describes someone who didn't get it, who never believed. The seed never took root in their lives. That one's easy.

Then comes the one ***sown on rocky ground***. In this one you can see the "borrower" or the "renter" we talked about earlier, who has no root in *himself*—all of the root was in others around him. So in this case of borrowed faith, when pressure comes, faith flies out the window. When the rubber hits the road and things get tough, your faith—not being yours to begin with—serves no purpose, gives no hope, and offers no help.

Next, the seeds ***sown among the thorns*** could be used to describe the one who picks and chooses. The seed finds earth, it digs in, but since its roots are entangled with the roots of thorns, the entanglement or the mixture of multiple beliefs that are inconsistent with each other chokes out faith. **When you pick and choose the parts of God that you want for yourself, you create another god—** one that cannot survive the worries of everyday life.

And finally, Jesus talks about a fourth landing place for the seeds, and that is ***the good ground***. In this case, the seed finds nice deep soil to bury itself in and take root, and since there are no weeds competing for the attention of the water and the sun, the seed can grow fat and happy and eventually spring up through the earth and climb toward the sun. In this case we see a seed that grows into a tree that then grows more seeds that fall to the ground and plants more trees. This kind of faith multiplies its fruit. It grows nourishment for those who come to it; it feeds them and makes them want more; and it speaks to the kindness and goodness of the One who sowed the seeds in the first place.

If you feel like your faith is on rocky ground and the thorns are fighting to rule your life, then your faith in God may be faltering or all together gone. You may feel Him to be ineffective, distant, unavailable—and because of that, you've given up on Him, or at least kept Him at arm's length. That's because the truth is that the seed of faith has yet to take root. **If your faith doesn't feel like your own, the truth might be that the seed never truly took root in your life.** That's good news—it means that the faith that you find ineffective, a failure, was never true faith at all. This just proves that faith in anything or anyone other than God is not faith at all. When your faith isn't your own, but another's, when you do not own it, it does not change you, it does not cost you, and it will not save you. And so knowing that, you can be done with the cheap imitation because it has proven to be of no value. **Believing what you have had until today was true faith and it just wasn't enough is the biggest lie you've ever believed.** True faith is powerful and life changing. Fake faith is ineffective and life sucking. But when the seed of faith falls onto good ground, when God clears away the weeds and you receive the seed, true faith can grow.

So let's take a look at what true faith looks like. Let's all start with the assumption that up until now you were living a lie, a pretend faith—one that looked and sounded real, but you know deep down was anything but genuine. Let's start from there and consider what it means to find your faith anew—to see it for what it really is for the first time as you start to consider giving up the charade and instead truly own your faith.

Owning Your Faith Will Save You

Christ can and will save a man who has been dishonest,
but He cannot save him while he is dishonest.

—A. W. TOZER

There once was a man who owned a piece of land. He decided that he would farm the land, and so he tilled the soil and then planted it with seeds. He knew the demand for corn crops was high and was sure that he would make a killing with his. As the season progressed, he ran out to check his thriving crop, and he started to question, "What kind of corn is this? Why isn't it growing high like corn

33

should?" He waited and waited, he weeded and weeded, he watered and watered, but day after day it started looking like he was getting something entirely different than corn. As he reached down to tug on his failure of a crop, he pulled so hard the root came out with the leaf and what he saw was not corn at all, but a carrot. Where did the man go wrong? What happened to his corn? Didn't he work the soil well enough? Didn't he water it when it was dry? Where did he go wrong? Of course the answer is obvious: it all started with the seed. He was tending to the wrong seed. This is exactly what happens in the lives of many people who start out believing or adhering to one thing and then end up believing they were either wrong or just plain ineffective at growing. This misunderstanding about what kind of seed took root is more common than you might think in the spiritual realm. And it can cause you to disown a faith that you never truly owned.

The Seeds of Faith

If you've lived on this earth for a decade or more, then the chances are that there have been many seeds sown in your life—many ways of thinking, many beliefs that have taken root and grown along with you. A lot of them might seem compatible with the seeds of faith in God, but as we saw in the parable of the sower, when other seeds compete in the same soil they can choke out the seeds of faith and can end up taking over your life. In order to truly own your faith, the seed of that faith has to take root in your life. And, like we've already seen, the soil where the seed falls is crucial in the growth of that seed. But now let's take a closer look at the seed of faith and the seeds that mimic that faith and deceive many into believing them to be something they are not.

Faith in Man

One of the most obvious seeds that gets sown early is the seed of faith, not in God but in man. Putting your faith in man starts at an early age when you naturally make an idol of your parents. When you were a small child, your parents could do no wrong. They were all-powerful, all-knowing, and all-loving, as far as you were concerned. You believed that they met all your needs, even if they didn't. And so they were your first exposure to the idea of God. But as a child grows, the godlikeness of the parents starts to be questioned. As you see them make mistakes, as they hurt you, disappoint you, or even spoil you, you start to see their humanity, and you begin to doubt the very person or people you used to put all of your faith in.

This doesn't negate the Word of God, but confirms it. As it says, "There is no one righteous, not even one. For all have sinned and fall short of the glory of God" (Rom. 3:10, 23). That means that **your parents cannot not mess up. They are *not* perfect like God, so they cannot be your God.** They cannot meet all your needs; they cannot always protect you; and they cannot always make you happy or even save you, because they, like you, are only human. For a lot of children, the failure of their parents to be perfect shakes their faith in God because, after all, it's usually from their parents that they first heard about Him. And when your parents fail to love you unconditionally, to forgive you completely, to understand you fully, to be patient with you always, or to give you grace repeatedly, your image of God can falter. That's because your faith was never truly in Him but in man. When the actions of a human being affect your faith in God, it's because you are confusing the two. For the child whose faith is borrowed or rented, any failure on the part of the actual owner of that faith negatively affects the borrower's faith. But when you own your own faith, the actions of others are seen through the light of God's goodness and not the other's badness. In other words, when God, not man, is your salvation and hope, then the actions of man are seen not as a weapon used against you but as a part of a far greater plan—a bigger picture that only the true God can see or conceive.

Seeing your parents—or anyone that you received your faith from—as human rather than divine sets you free to not only forgive them but to love them. The trouble with the mistakes parents make is that the children either accuse them of not being good enough parents or accuse themselves of not being lovable enough. But neither is true. Rather, humans are not capable of perfection; they all are as weak, lonely, fearful, and sinful as you are—they just try to hide it most of the time. This act of hiding our failure and our sinfulness leads to great turmoil as those around us see the hypocrisy in our pasted-on smiles or hypocritical faith. And while hypocrisy might be a systemic problem within the church, it doesn't have to become your problem. The hypocrisy of man, again, just speaks to the validity of God's Word (see Ps. 51:4). There is no one who is righteous, so why are we so surprised when the people we love prove their humanity? Shouldn't we just let their humanity confirm His divinity?

➡ **Michael's Hypocritical Faith:** I used to say I loved God, but my life—first private then public— betrayed my hypocrisy. For what we talk about, what we obsess over, what dominates our most intimate thoughts and motivates our most subtle actions, it is that which we truly and deeply love. And so my deep desire to get married and have kids, to have an obsessive love affair like my parents did, to be a successful and respected college coach, and to live in comfort were my true loves. God was simply my taxi driver who took me to my mistress's house. But God tolerates no rivals, and all other loves eventually fail to satisfy, leaving you empty. So as my relationships failed, as I left jobs in disgrace, there was one ignored and marginalized love that still remained—the Father of the prodigal waiting with open arms.

My life is now a daily testimony to the grace offered to all us hypocrites, not as someone who has arrived as hypocrisy-free, but as one who daily has to put to death all those vastly inferior loves and rest in a new affection. God's love and mercy for hypocrites is new every morning. Don't let hypocrites like me convince you of the absence of God, but let my existence drive you to the reality that you no longer have to be perfect to be loved by God. People are always going to pass themselves off as perfect without the peace and grace of God. Take joy in the fact that God delights in using imperfect people to accomplish His will and purpose. ◄—

The Bible repeatedly uses examples of this kind of human failure and God's sovereignty to encourage believers to not rely on others to either define them or to save them. One of the best examples of this is the life of Joseph. You've heard of him and his amazing Technicolor coat. He was favored by his dad and hated by his brothers. So much so that they got rid of him, sold him into slavery, and told dear old dad he was dead. Life went from worse to worser for Joseph as he worked diligently as a slave but was accused of wrongdoing when he ticked off his boss's wife for brushing off her advances. For that honorable nonresponse, he ended up in jail. Throughout all the trials of Joseph's life, he could have blamed a lot of people. He could have had a miniseries made about his life called *Revenge*, but he needed no such thing. Instead, he looked to the perfect One to be God, to be sovereign, and not to man. And so when he had the chance to save all of his brothers from the famine in their land, he took it rather than allowing them to starve. This is what he said to their bewildered faces: "You meant evil against me, but God meant it for good, to bring it about that many people should be kept alive, as they are today" (Gen. 50:20 ESV).

Faith in Yourself

When the evidence of the failure of man to be perfect presents itself in your life, a common reaction to it is often rejection of your faith in man and his God, in exchange for faith in self. As people disappoint and hurt you, you begin to develop a worldview that attempts to protect you from any future pain. This mind-set determines your thoughts and feelings and demands that you adhere to a set of laws that were created in reaction to the suffering that you determined can never happen again. This law functions similarly to God's law. In it you have decided things like:

- "I will never trust them again."
- "I won't be made a fool of."
- "If they cross me, I'll get even."

The hurtful or just plain stupid actions of others shape your beliefs, your dreams, and your fears. And in that environment, **you determine the only way to be safe is to reject difficult or unkind people and to live for yourself.**

Even if you have never been hurt but have had a blessed life, you can still develop a worldview that makes your comfort, your feelings, your hopes, your dreams, and your fears the focus of your life. As that happens, your actions reflect your self-will, and your faith centers on your happiness over God's. So **when He asks for things that infringe upon your self-made law of revenge, of self-protection, or self-promotion, then you must reject Him in favor of your deeply felt principles and belief in looking out for number one.**

This can even show up in tandem with the life of faith. That happens when you believe in Jesus and you love God, but you also believe there is something for you to do yourself in order to get God's love and forgiveness. A lot of people refer to this as works, the act of working for your salvation. Your faith, in this instance, isn't fully in the saving power of Christ, but has the added zip of faith in your ability to do what God wants in order to please Him. People who live with this paradigm believe in God but determine His acceptance to be based on the goodness or badness of their actions. So, **for many the statement "I'm a good person" carries the same amount of weight as "Jesus died for me."** This betrays the presence of not only the seed of faith in God but of faith in self, and so we see a garden growing two different things.

In Matthew 13:24–30, Jesus tells another seed parable, and this one explains just what we are talking about here. In this parable the farmer has planted wheat, but in the night his enemies have come in and planted a weed called a "darnel." This weed is very clever because it looks exactly like wheat when it first sprouts, and an expert can barely tell the difference, but once these weeds are full-grown and are ground into flour, they are poisonous. It's no coincidence that Jesus' parables on seeds are consistent about faith in God being grown as a singular crop, not sharing its soil with faith in anything other than God Himself.

But that's exactly what you try to do when you put your faith in yourself. Whether you believe that you can control your own destiny, obey the law, prove yourself worthy enough, or that looking out for number one is the only way to assure your success, you have put your faith in someone who cannot succeed. You can work and plan all you want, but you are like an ant trying to move a rubber tree plant—powerless. As you can read in God's Word, "The heart of man plans his way, but the LORD establishes his steps" (Prov. 16:9 ESV). And, "A person cannot receive even one thing unless it is given him from heaven" (John 3:27 ESV).

➡ **Hayley's Weedy Faith:** I love the law, I love it!! It makes sense, it's comforting, and I can tell you everything that you need to do in order to be holy. I am an obedience junkie. But I found something terrible at work in my addiction to law, and that was the stress and worry of not being good enough. No matter how much I try—and believe me, I've tried—I cannot keep the entire law. In fact, I can't keep it for one day. And I am really driven and really obedient. But my nature, just like everyone's, is to sin, thanks to Adam and Eve, and so God is proved right again, every time I mess up. Not that this gives me permission to mess up more in order to prove Him wrong; that's illogical. But the most important words for me to remember as I learn what pleases God is that there is no condemnation for those who are in Christ (see Rom. 8:1). Without knowing this, you can end up putting all of your faith in yourself, like I did, in order to be good enough for God and good enough to make it to heaven. Accepting the fact that I can't do it, that I can't save myself, actually leads to my ultimate salvation in Christ. ◄

Faith in yourself always ultimately disappoints because you cannot be perfect. As long as you look to yourself to save yourself, to redeem yourself, to change yourself, to protect or comfort yourself, you will have trouble. Sure, you may succeed for awhile, but the time will come when you will fail, and when you fail, where will you turn?

The seeds of self once planted grow only the fruit of the flesh—after all, that is what they rely on, the flesh. So the seeds you feed and water will ultimately destroy you. Things like fear, doubt, worry, stress, bitterness, hatred, isolation, resentment, fighting, sexual immorality, and addiction grow on the branches of the tree that comes from the seed of self. Those emotions that plague you and control you grew because you believed at one point that they would protect or save you. They offered you a plentiful garden paradise but will entangle you with a weed-riddled and fruitless land.

Faith in Happiness

God's goal isn't to make you happy; it's to make you holy. But so many times Christians and non-Christians alike believe that happiness is the goal of life, and so when the happy doesn't come, life looks like it's breaking down. But **happiness was never meant to be the objective, but rather the symptom.** Huh? Confused yet? Let's clear the air. How many times have you believed that God was punishing you? That He was yanking the rug out from under you? Tempting you? Or just plain ignoring you? When you believe that your lack of happiness is an indictment on God's goodness, it's easy for your faith to be choked. It's easy to think He's a bad Father because He's not holding up His end of the deal. But His end of the deal isn't your happiness, but your perfection, and sometimes suffering and trials are the only path to that perfection.

Think about it for a minute: who has more wisdom, more grace, more kindness—someone who has had the good life, gotten whatever they wanted, whenever they wanted it, or someone who has been through a lot of struggle and come out the other side? God's Word makes it clear suffering isn't a punishment from God to be dreaded, but something to be thankful for. As it says in Romans 5:3–4, "We rejoice in our sufferings, knowing that suffering produces endurance, and endurance produces character, and character produces hope" (ESV). **Believing that your suffering proves God to be a liar and a jerk is inconsistent with what He says about the life of faith.** Your suffering was allowed in order to perfect you, not to leave you in your messy life. That's why James can say, "Count it all joy, my brothers, when you meet trials of various kinds, for you know that the testing of your faith produces steadfastness. And let steadfastness have its full effect, that you may be perfect and complete, lacking in nothing" (James 1:2–4 ESV). The truth is that suffering is the catalyst for change and growth. Just like the butterfly must suffer in order to break free from his cocoon or his wings will never be strong enough to fly, so your suffering serves a great purpose, but only when you allow it to serve you. When you hate it or fear it, then you empower it for evil rather than good. In other words, you allow it to destroy you rather than to grow you.

Change is an essential part of life; **if you aren't in the process of changing, then you are dying, not growing.** And suffering brings the change you need in order to perfect your life. But if your faith is in happiness, then suffering is your archenemy and you will do all you can to avoid it. But by so doing, you avoid the very thing that God wants to use to remake you in the image of Christ.

Faith in Idols

Slow down! Don't skip over this section because you don't have a shrine in your house or haven't melted all your gold into the shape of a cow that you worship. Idols aren't what they used to be; they've matured, grown, kept up with the times, and they are more easily available now than they have ever been.

An idol is something you have devoted your life to. It might be a way of life that involves self-sacrifice, self-discipline, or self-obsession. It might involve devotion to money, success, comfort, power, more stuff, less stuff, fame, friends, animals, even church. The bottom line is that idolatry happens when you obsess. When there is something in your life that you are consumed with, that you can't live without, or that you would do anything to keep—if you love something with all of your heart—then you have an idol. We can say that because of what Jesus said in Matthew 22:37: "Love the Lord your God with all your heart and with all your soul and with all your mind" (ESV). That means you were made to obsess, to give 100 percent of your everything to Him. So when you obsess over anything other than God, you make that thing your little god, your idol, and God is replaced.

It might seem like God can share the stage of your heart with your dreams and passions, but God demands your full devotion, not in order to control or punish you but to save you. In our book *Obsessed*, we talked about this way of looking at idolatry: when you obsess over something or someone, you start out just loving it, but over time you start to think you need it. Then you begin making sacrifices for it, giving up stuff, even your morals, in order to get what you want. You cut corners, make compromises, sacrifice for your obsession. And so you look for others who obsess over the same things you obsess over— we call that *fellowship*, hanging out with fellow "believers," talking about or doing what you all love. With this comes the need to share your passion with others, to talk about it, to witness to it. And like a missionary, you set out to convert as many people as you can, not to faith in Jesus, but to your obsession. In the end, you end up controlled by your obsession, passion, or dream. We learn in 2 Peter 2:19 that "you are a slave to whatever controls you" (NLT). So you become a slave to the very thing that you adore. But slavery has a great deal to do with faith. Jesus explained it this way: "No one can serve two masters, for either he will hate the one and love the other, or he will be devoted to the one and despise the other" (Matt. 6:24 ESV).

Why don't you own your faith? Because **you cannot be a part-time slave.** You will be controlled by whatever you focus your life on. The Olympic gymnast is consumed with his sport, day and night. The medical student is consumed with her practice. The things in life that you invest in take up your time as well as your heart. **When you are consumed with anything or anyone other than God, then you have created for yourself an idol,** and in that you have disowned the one true God. So does this mean that we all must become monks and avoid outside pursuits? Not at all! What it means is that we must do all we do for the glory of God out of our obsessed love of God that grows out of His unconditional love for us.

Whatever you go to for the things that God has said He would do is the object of your worship. So **if you go to food to comfort you, guns to protect you, people to validate or save you, then you worship the creation**

rather than the Creator. The seeds of idolatry choke out faith. Jesus' words must ring in your ears; you cannot serve two masters. If you believe you can, then we can guarantee that the master you serve is not God, but another smaller god, an idol of your own making.

Only One Faith Saves You

Whether you have put your faith in man, in yourself, in your happiness, or in an idol, if you've lived long at all you've seen that faith tested. You've seen it fail you and you've had to make a decision to keep on keeping on or to look somewhere else to put your faith. That's because we all need something to believe in, in order to save us from the difficulties and pains of life. If you've walked away from your faith in God, or at the very least ignored it, then you've probably seen little in the way of salvation in your life. Now we aren't talking about the salvation that gets you into those pearly gates; that's one kind of salvation. You've probably already heard about that kind of salvation more times than you can count—the saving work of Jesus on the cross, His dying for your sins so that they will no longer be counted against you by a holy God who won't allow evil into paradise. But the salvation we want to talk about is far more immediate, and that is the salvation from sin. **Jesus didn't come just to save you for heaven but to save you from sin's power.** This is amazing; check it out. Don't just skip this part; it's revolutionary—even to someone who's heard the whole salvation story over and over again:

> Don't you know that when you offer yourselves to
> someone to obey him as slaves, you are slaves to
> the one whom you obey—whether you are slaves to
> sin, which leads to death, or to obedience, which
> leads to righteousness? But thanks be to God that,
> though you used to be slaves to sin, you whole-
> heartedly obeyed the form of teaching to which you
> were entrusted. You have been set free from sin and
> have become slaves to righteousness. I put this in
> human terms because you are weak in your natural
> selves. Just as you used to offer the parts of your
> body in slavery to impurity and to ever-increasing
> wickedness, so now offer them in slavery to righ-
> teousness leading to holiness. (Rom. 6:16–19 NIV)

Did you get all that? It's the same slave master stuff we talked about in the idol section. Before you give your life to Christ, you are a slave to sin. Period. The end. We all are slaves to sin before we accept the blood of Jesus as our salvation. But once we accept His death as sufficient to cover us, we are set free from sin. Wow! Did you know that? Have you been set free? Or are you still enslaved to your emotions, by anger, by depression, by worry? Do you want to be free from addiction and fear? Then owning your faith is the answer. When you own your faith, you turn your life over to God to own you. And when that happens, you are set free from the powerful grip that sin used to have on you. Does it mean that you never sin again? No, that would mean you were sinless, and we've already covered that; no one is sinless. But, it does mean that you are no longer enslaved to sin. We don't need to go into that. You can think for yourself about whatever controls you, sin or not. If it isn't God, then you are in bondage to something that wants to destroy you. But Jesus has made a way for you to be free from sin. The most amazing words on this topic are found in Romans 6. We've already given you some of them, but why not give you more? Take the time to let these verses sink in.

> What should we say then? Should we continue in
> sin so that grace may multiply? Absolutely not!
> How can we who died to sin still live in it? Or
> are you unaware that all of us who were baptized
> into Christ Jesus were baptized into His death?
> Therefore we were buried with Him by baptism
> into death, in order that, just as Christ was raised
> from the dead by the glory of the Father, so we too

may walk in a new way of life. For if we have been joined with Him in the likeness of His death, we will certainly also be in the likeness of His resurrection. For we know that our old self was crucified with Him in order that sin's dominion over the body may be abolished, so that we may no longer be enslaved to sin, since a person who has died is freed from sin's claims. Now if we died with Christ, we believe that we will also live with Him, because we know that Christ, having been raised from the dead, will not die again. Death no longer rules over Him. For in light of the fact that He died, He died to sin once for all; but in light of the fact that He lives, He lives to God. So, you too consider yourselves dead to sin but alive to God in Christ Jesus. Therefore do not let sin reign in your mortal body, so that you obey its desires. And do not offer any parts of it to sin as weapons for unrighteousness. But as those who are alive from the dead, offer yourselves to God, and all the parts of yourselves to God as weapons for righteousness. For sin will not rule over you, because you are not under law but under grace. (Rom. 6:1–14)

So much here, so very much! Let's see if we can break it down. When you recognize Jesus is the Lord of your life and are baptized, thus confirming in front of witnesses that He is your God, you are symbolizing and testifying that you are figuratively buried with Him. Why? So that you can walk in a new way of life. That's because your old self is crucified with Him, thus killing sin's rule over you. We know that because God's Word tells us that the person who has died is free from sin's claims. So believers can consider themselves dead to sin because they are no longer under law but under grace. When you needed the law to save you, through your good works, you were under that law. And if you messed up on any part of it, then you failed it all. There's no passing grade for a 99 percent. But when you took on the blood of Jesus, you went from being under the law to under grace. That is, God no longer looks at your works and judges you by the law but gives you forgiveness freely; all He asks is your agreement with Him that you have sinned. This is called confession (see 1 John 1:9).

So for the person who is willing to own their faith there is not only salvation for heaven but also salvation from sin. That means that as you begin to see the areas in your life where you are controlled by something or someone, you can turn them over to God, forsake your idol, give yourself to Him, and be set free. **For the believer, there is no addiction, only sin.** When you call your addiction sin, it empowers you to walk away from it, to reject it, and it gives you the power of God on your side. As we see in 2 Peter 1:3: "His divine power has granted to us all things that pertain to life and godliness, through the knowledge of him who called us to his own glory and excellence" (ESV).

If your faith isn't saving you from sin, if you aren't making progress toward more and more freedom, then it might be because you do not own a saving faith, but an imitation of faith. But if you are willing to own it, to define yourself by it, to dive in headfirst and to trust Him with your every move, then you will experience more salvation than you've ever known before.

Growing Your Faith

God gives you all of His gifts in seed form. That means you don't start out a mighty oak, but you start in the darkness of the earth, dying and then rising again as you reach toward the sun. So you cannot expect your life to be all you ever imagined in one day. Your faith will grow when you are mindful to pull the weeds that you have let grow along next to it. God delights when you dig up your obsessions and turn them over to Him. It's not that God doesn't want you to be passionate and to love your life; He just wants you to be passionate for Him and to love what He has given you to do.

When you are doing what God has given you to do, your passion overflows. You can hardly wait to get up in the morning. You aren't weighed down by the cares of the world because you live to serve only Him. He is your obsession, and as your obsession, He never disappoints. The Bible makes it clear that God is sovereign—He is in control of this world. Many people give too much credit to the Devil, saying he is trying to stop them, to change them, to control them. But the truth is, when you turn your life over to God, the Devil can't touch you. He's powerless in the life of the believer except that God allows him in, as can be seen in the life of Job (see Job 1:6–12). And if God allows him to do a work, it is for a great purpose.

God is sovereign—His will will be done. Like it says in Isaiah 46:9–10: "Remember what happened long ago, for I am God, and there is no other; I am God, and no one is like Me. I declare the end from the beginning, and from long ago what is not yet done, saying: My plan will take place, and I will do all My will." **When you own your faith, His will becomes your will.** When that happens, you are always successful because His will will always be done. That doesn't mean that life will be perfect, but you can guarantee that even when things look bleak, God is in control. Even when life hurts, God is good.

It is essential in the life of faith to know and trust the sovereignty of God. If God is not sovereign, then that would mean there is someone who can go against Him, beat Him, overcome Him. In that case He is not God at all, but a weak being that cannot achieve His will. This is not the God of the Bible. The God of the Bible is all-powerful, all-knowing, and sovereign. He is not absent and not looking away, but is actively involved on this earth, saving those who put their faith in His hands. When you own your faith, God reaches down and saves you from being separated from Him and His love.

"In all these things we are more than victorious through Him who loved us. For I am persuaded that not even death or life, angels or rulers, things present or things to come, hostile powers, height or depth, or any other created thing will have the power to separate us from the love of God that is in Christ Jesus our Lord!" (Rom. 8:37–39).

Owning Your Faith Will Cost You

When Christ calls a man, he bids him come and die.
—DIETRICH BONHOEFFER

When Hayley bought her first house, she was scared to death. As soon as she unlocked the door and walked in, buyer's remorse hit like a speeding train. "What have I done?" she cried. The fear of commitment hurt like the sting of thousands of bees, and as she walked around the empty rooms, the cost began to ring up in her heart. What demands would this house bring? How would she possibly meet them all? What had she done? The cost of ownership is a jagged little pill that can have the nasty side effect of angst and doubt when it comes to the big commitments in life. In order to fully commit—to marry yourself to a major life choice—you have to first assess the cost. Can you afford it? Will you freak out or run out? How much of yourself are you willing to give up? Commitment requires assessment. As Jesus said in Luke, "Which of you, wanting to build a tower, doesn't first sit down and calculate the cost to see if he has enough to complete it?" In the same way, therefore, every one of you who does not say good-bye to all his possessions cannot be My disciple" (Luke 14:28, 33).

If these words don't freak you out a little, then you haven't yet considered the cost of owning your faith. But then again, if they *do* freak you out, it can be easy to plug your ears and look for other feel-good verses that sound better to your heart. But deep down you can't get away from the fact that **total commitment means giving up some things that you might not want to give up.**

That's not just true in the spiritual realm, but in every other area of life. When you commit to a dream, a relationship, a career, you commit to a price that will often require you to give up good stuff so you can get to great stuff. When you really value something, you will go to great lengths to keep it. You know it's true. Success in anything doesn't come with partial commitment, but with diving in headfirst. And when you take a leap of faith, it will cost you more than the ground underneath you— often costing you much of what you love.

Anything in your life that is inconsistent with faith in God is the price that you must pay to follow Him. As we said earlier, when you own something, truly own it, it owns you. So it's no coincidence that Jesus calls His disciples to say good-bye to all of their possessions. What God doesn't want is for you is to be a slave to the stuff of this world. He wants you to be free, and He knows that all those things that you possess, that you are afraid to give up, really possess you. In fact, all of the struggles in your life—all of the strain, the worry, the fear—all of it comes from the things that you are afraid to give up. So let's take a look at some of those things that war against your faith and must be sacrificed in order for you to Own It.

Time

The single most valuable commodity in your life is time. What you do with it determines not only what you become but who you are. **The cost of ownership always includes time.** If you own a dog, you have to give him your time. If you own a house, that means a lot of your

59

time has to go into just keeping it up. Want to become a doctor? It will take a lot of your time. Want a healthy relationship with someone? Then you have to spend time with that person. And you cannot truly own your faith if you do not give God your time.

One of the things that make Christianity different from other religions is that it is a relationship. And relationships aren't like trinkets you buy and put on your shelf and only glance at as you walk past them on your way to doing other things. They need a significant amount of time. In fact, **the amount of time your relationships get points to the health and depth of those relationships.** If you say you are in love with a person whom you met once but haven't spent more than a few minutes a week with since, you are deceiving yourself. True love compels you to spend your time with the one you love. If you don't spend time, then clearly your relationship isn't as strong as you thought.

It's not just a coincidence that Jesus calls Himself the Bread of Life. God is like food; you need Him every day. You can't get Him all on Sunday and be filled up for the next six days. You need to eat daily. When the Israelites wandered in the desert, God sent them manna, a bread-like substance that rained down from the sky each day. It is interesting and applicable to note that if they saved any manna for the next day, it would be rotten by morning. Each day the people had to go back to God for the food they needed; it couldn't be stored up. If you believe that you can store up your relationship with God, and find no need to go out each day and meet Him for your manna, then your faith will be anemic and weak, if not dead. No, the cost of ownership—the price of faith—is your time. You must decide if your time, both mentally and physically, is worth spending on God, daily coming to Him for the spiritual food you need. As you spend time in God's Word, prayerfully asking Him to speak through His Word, you will be spiritually fed and find yourself drawing closer and closer to Him. **The degree God intervenes in your life will be directly proportional to the time you spend with Him.** Not that He doesn't intervene in the lives of the distant, but those who are distant are less likely to recognize His hand than those who are close to Him. That is why people who fail to spend time with God break under pressure—they fail when times get tough; they freak out, lose control, fall to temptation—all because they don't know God enough or spend enough time with Him to know what He is doing in their lives. Then when something bad happens, they are unable to associate it with His love—they take it as an assault, a tragedy, or a struggle. But when you turn to Him each morning—when you make your day center around Him and His will—you know exactly where He is and where you are, and in that perfect place nothing can harm you and nothing can beat you.

How naive to think that you can live your life for God without first dedicating your life to Him each morning! Morning is the best time because it sets the tone for your entire day. It defines your choices, your pace, your emotions, your priorities. When you start each day off as Jesus started His, in the presence of the Father, not only does your faith grow, but your day belongs to God, and with that all of the things that happen in that day. What a safe and wonderful feeling to know that your moment-by-moment rests in the hands of the Father.

Control

Turning your life over to someone, even to God, is a scary prospect when you aren't sure that He even knows what He's doing. After all, you know what's best for you. You have desires, things you can't live without, and you know their value, but for some reason God just doesn't totally get it. In this tug of war with your heart, it can be easy to think that God's a big bully, come to take everything and everyone you love—that His goal is your complete submission through control. But that's an improper understanding of our God. In 1 John 4:8 we learn a really important fact about God: "God is love." That means that everything He does is in your best interest. His love for you compels everything He does and so He can be trusted. And because He is omnipotent, all-powerful (see Isa. 40:28), and all-knowing (see Heb. 4:13), He can actually do whatever He wants (see Isa. 46:9–10). Being God makes Him the final say in everything. No one can interrupt Him, defeat Him, or derail Him (see Dan. 4:35). So putting your trust in God to not just be present in your life but to manage the world around you and to take care of those things you have always thought you had to control is the smartest thing you can do.

But controlling your life and the world around you is your job! You've done it for so long, and you actually like it. Control, or the illusion of control, feels good. It feels like you are doing something. And the idea of giving up your attempt at control sounds dangerous. After all, can you really trust that God will do all that you would do in His shoes? **If you struggle with wanting to be in control, of needing to manage not only your life but the lives of those around you, then what you are doing is playing God.** That's right, you've found that He's just too slow on the draw, too disinterested, or otherwise too busy to play a part in your little life. And so in order to supplement His work, you've stepped in yourself to manage and control things the way they need to be controlled. This idea of control makes God a nonevent, a nonentity, and puts Him instead in the category of self-help guru or decorative idol. And from this position you will never own your faith because your faith is more deeply rooted in yourself than in Him.

This idea of control affects what you fear, worry about, and obsess over. That's because when the world rests on your shoulders, your load is heavy. In this role of all-powerful, you can buckle under the strain of supporting a world you were never meant to support. But faith, **true faith, costs you the luxury of control.** God doesn't yank it from your hands, but asks you to loosen your grip and drop it yourself. As long as you fight for control, you are choosing your will over God's, but Jesus taught us how to pray, "Your will be done." And that's the prayer of faith, "Your will, not mine." This idea means complete freedom. It takes the need to manage life off of your plate and puts it all on God's. It takes your weakness and trades it in for His strength (see 2 Cor. 12:7–10). This idea rejects the illusion that you could make your will happen anyway and, instead, trusts that His will is far better.

Imagining that ultimately you have any control over

your world at all is a grand delusion. One of the best words on this comes from Lamentations 3:37–38, which says, "Who is there who speaks and it happens, unless the Lord has ordained it? Do not both adversity and good come from the mouth of the Most High?" See, **nothing happens except that God allows it.** And believing that you need to control the situation, especially when things appear to be out of control, neuters your faith and leaves it ineffective.

This cost of faith is high. It is going to feel like more than you can afford, a spiritual taking-your-hands-off-the-wheel, that can seem like a recipe for disaster. But the old cliché of making God your copilot keeps you ultimately in charge, with Him just barking directions. But getting out of the driver seat and allowing Him to drive your life is the true definition of faith. **As long as you are behind the wheel, you are playing God with your life and the lives of those around you.**

➡ **Michael's Quest for Control:** I love being in control. If some buddies and I are going to lunch, I've got to drive. If I'm speaking at a conference and an event organizer offers to book my flight and hotel, I say, "No thanks" and book it myself. Yes, I love me some control. This even plays out in my marriage with Hayley. In the first years of our marriage, any time she did something, even the smallest thing, that wasn't how I would do it, I would ~~correct teach adjust~~ **control** her into complying with my will of how life should be lived. Ah, marital bliss! But as patient as she was and as compliant as she was, I realized that she was never going to be perfect; I never would be able to control her. And so slowly, far too slowly for Hayley most likely, I realized that my law of control was me trying to be God yet not being able to live up to my own standards. I'm so thankful for a forgiving wife but even more for a forgiving God that has everything under control. For when I try and control my life (and those in it), my life is full of stress and strife. But when I surrender my illusion of control to Him, I find a peace that surpasses all understanding. ◀━

Your Law

The law is a comforting thing. It sets boundaries and promises protection from going too fast or being too stupid. That's why we create laws of our own. Whenever you say things like "I'll do whatever it takes to _____," or "I'll never let _____ happen again," you are laying down your law—a law that you vow never to break because it was designed to protect you, to control your future, and to avoid failure. Of course, God's law is fine for you until it crosses your law and you're left with a choice: whose law will you break, and whose will you follow? It's so easy when God demands something of you that sounds dangerous to reject in favor of your own law. Like when someone hates you and God says to "love your enemies," you are left with a quandary: will you emotionally "turn the other cheek," or will you dig in your heels and fight, get them back, protect yourself? Which law you go with shows who your God really is.

Face it, we all have those unwritten rules that we live by as a safety valve for God's law. But **faith in God will cost your own law.** And subconsciously you know that giving up those things that you said you would never do, or that you have always worked to protect against, fought to get, are dying to have, will not only cost you control, but might even cost you pain, loss, or failure. And **when that's too high a price to pay, then God's sovereignty is rejected in favor of your own.**

But it's all an illusion. The notion that your law assures not only your safety but your success is a lie. That's because at the heart of your law isn't holiness, goodness, or even righteousness, but selfishness. After all, your law was ultimately written with one thing in mind: you.

That is the definition of selfish—being all about you. Even when your law seems to be based on your desire to protect those whom you love, ultimately it's about protecting you from losing them. Your laws serve to prove a very important thing: your self-obsession. When you are self-obsessed, you run all of your choices and beliefs through the filter of yourself. You make all of your decisions, even your kind and loving ones, with the continual thought toward yourself. And in that self-obsessed state, you rely on yourself to determine right from wrong, to make the best sacrifices, to give the proper rewards, and to lay down the best punishment. Now do these ideas remind you of anything? Determining morality, choosing sacrifice, exacting punishment. See it? See how that's all God's job? In taking it on yourself, you are playing God—pretending perfection, feigning complete power, acting all-knowing, believing you can be present everywhere you need to be in order to control the world around you. But if you were honest with yourself, you would agree that it is impossible for you to be perfect, omnipotent, omniscient, and omnipresent, because you are, after all, only human. But your self-obsession says otherwise as it lives to serve yourself, to honor yourself, and even to judge yourself.

Your Guilt

There is only one judge and that is God. Unfortunately a lot of us believe that His judgment isn't as good as ours, and so in this pretend world where we are our own gods, we get really good at judging guilt from innocence. Even when you know that God is the ultimate judge, it can still be easy to make up your mind that His judgment is too lenient. After all, He offers forgiveness with nothing more than a confession and a repentant heart (see 1 John 1:9). But how many times do you think that more is demanded, that some other punishment is warranted? How many times do you decide that your own guilt is particularly stubborn and requires more than a simple confession? And so you give a new ruling; instead of "not guilty," you decide that guilt will remain till penance is paid. So deeply do you understand the failure on your part to be perfect that you feel a strong need for there to be justice. You sentence yourself to the hard labor of working to fix the mess you've made, to the punishment of hurting yourself in order to set the balance of justice right again, and to the discipline of self-inflicted penance. Whatever the verdict, you are certain that justice must be met in order for you to be set free.

The trouble with all of this justice stuff is that it tends to take your self-made law and create self-made guilt.

See, God gave you a sense of conviction in order to save you from the stupid stuff of sin. When this conviction comes, its job is to make you sad, to make you feel bad for the sin in your life, and that bad feeling makes you want to repent, to confess and stop doing whatever it was you were doing. That's good guilt, and it's healthy, and easily covered up by the grace of God (see 2 Cor. 7:10). In other words, at the point of confession it is finished, no more guilt, nothing to worry or obsess about. But the bad kind of guilt operates under a different set of beliefs. Unlike good guilt, bad guilt doesn't offer you forgiveness. It doesn't drive you closer to God but farther away from Him. If you feel guilt in your life that you believe is too much for God to forgive, then you are letting bad guilt feed the idea that your law is more important than God's. That your ideas on guilt and punishment are more precise and just than His since you demand punishment more fitting of the crime than He does. This only feeds your desire to play God as it encourages your supremacy over Him in the area of justice and punishment.

If you have confessed your sins to God, He has forgiven you. You can be assured of that. But if you still feel guilty, then you have not fully understood the cost of owning your faith. In order to pay the price, you must give up your right to be more just than God. **You must give**

up your right to hold on to your guilt and to punish yourself. Holding on to these rights distances you from God, making your will more important than His, and leaves your faith in Him damaged and anemic. In order to be more just than God, you must be more holy, righteous, and good, and know the end from the beginning (see Isa. 46:10), the eternal purpose for things (see Eph. 3:11), and then, and only then, can you say that your sense of justice is better than His.

Justice

When you are bent on justice, you can judge not only yourself with vigor but others as well. The world isn't fair, life is hard, and so justice becomes your cry. You see unfairness and determine to balance the scales. And so when someone sins, you spring to action to level the playing field by retribution, revenge, or punishment. As the purveyor of all that is just, you find the need to struggle against the world in order to fix it. But what you are failing to recognize is that we all deserve punishment because there is no one righteous, not one single one (see Rom. 3:10). We all are messed up, failing and hurting one another, so is it any wonder that people fail you, that they fail each other and even the world? And can you honestly

71

say that you are capable of balancing the scales of justice and so save the world? That job can only be done by someone who is perfect, who has the power and the ability to do it—and that is God Himself.

What we all fail to recognize when we demand punishment for the sins of others is that God hasn't punished us for all of our sins. Surely we can count many of our own sins, failures, and lacking. And surely we deserve far greater punishment than we have been given. But God hasn't struck us down; He hasn't plagued us or even rejected us. He stands with open arms offering us the grace that was afforded by the only sacrifice that could be made for the sinful world, you included—His own Son. This grace He offers isn't meant to end with you. He gives it to you so that you can give it to others. **His divine act of not holding your sin against you because of His Son should be all the fuel you need to not hold the weaknesses and failures of others against them.** Not that you can't judge between right and wrong, you can, but taking that a step further and exacting punishment for the sins of others is arrogant, to say the least. That means your attempts to get revenge—to hurt others because of the evil they have done, to treat them the way their sins deserve—makes you not more just than God, but more selfish. Because having been freely forgiven by God, you now stand demanding more of others than He demands of you.

In a world where man's justice is considered better than God's, we would have never had a savior that went to the cross because no one who loved Him would have allowed Him to suffer for the sins He never committed. **Man's sense of fairness makes the cross impossible because grace is completely unfair, imbalanced,** and doesn't allow the punishment to be laid where the punishment is deserved. But thank God He is not human and we are not God. His justice is perfect, and in it He provides for the forgiveness of all our sins, even the ones we believe deserve much worse than His grace.

Jesus explains this broken sense of justice in the parable of the unforgiving servant. He tells about a servant who owes his king a ton of money. But after begging for patience, the king gives it to him and forgives the loan. The servant then walks out and bumps into another servant who owes him a buck or two and starts to strangle him. When the poor guy asks for patience, the first servant says, "Forget it," and totes him off to jail. When the king gets wind of the story, he is furious with the servant who just a few minutes earlier was forgiven thousands more. The king takes back his forgiveness and locks the guy up in jail to be tortured until every penny is paid. At the end of the story, Jesus says this: "So My heavenly Father will also do to you if each of you does not forgive his brother from his heart" (Matt. 18:35).

When your law, fueled by your sense of justice, refuses to offer forgiveness or grace to the world around you and even to accept it yourself, the faith you have isn't in God but in yourself. So rather than owning your faith, you own your sins and the sins of the world as you attempt to balance the scales of justice to suit you and to serve your will. But God asks you to give up the management of sin in your life to Him. He asks you to lay it down and to walk away from your god-complex and instead to surrender justice to Him just as Jesus did, who "when He was reviled, He did not revile in return; when He was suffering, He did not threaten but entrusted Himself to the One who judges justly" (1 Pet. 2:23). **Trusting God to be good enough or fair enough comes with the territory of faith.** If you are unwilling to trust Him, then you will be left with the infirmity that Jesus came to take away.

Isaiah 53:4–6 puts the justice of God seen in the cross like this:

> Yet He Himself bore our sicknesses, and He carried
> our pains; but we in turn regarded Him stricken,
> struck down by God, and afflicted. But He was
> pierced because of our transgressions, crushed

because of our iniquities; punishment for our peace was on Him, and we are healed by His wounds. We all went astray like sheep; we all have turned to our own way; and the LORD has punished Him for the iniquity of us all.

As long as you demand justice for the sins of others, you reject the cross that already paid the price for sin. As we read in Romans 5:6–8, "Christ died for the ungodly. For rarely will someone die for a just person—though for a good person perhaps someone might even dare to die. But God proves His own love for us in that while we were still sinners, Christ died for us!" Demanding justice, payback, retribution, makes Christ's death insufficient and sets you to work to even the score. But faith in Christ will cost you your sense of justice. When you own your faith, you let go of judging others and enforcing the punishment you deem fit, and instead you overflow with the same grace that God poured into you.

Your Rights

Your self-made law and your feelings about your personal rights are intricately linked. In fact, the foundation of all of the laws you place on yourself, all of your self-imposed rules, stem from your sense of what is right for

75

you. It goes against human nature to choose what is wrong for yourself. Even the self-injurer hurts herself because she believes it is the right thing for her. The rights you believe belong to you inform your decisions and your feelings. They are foundational to your moral compass and your beliefs about you and your relationship with those around you.

The things that you label as rights are an indicator of where you put your faith. If you believe your rights to be the right to life, liberty, and the pursuit of happiness, then you must put your faith in the political system that promises those rights will be protected. If you stand on your right to do whatever you want to with your body, then your faith is in yourself and your ability to decide right from wrong. If you believe in the right to protect yourself from invaders, then your faith may be put into your security system or gun cabinet. Your idea of the rights you have as a human being speak to things that you deem the most important in this world. They point to your priorities and define where you draw the line, where you start to make demands. In other words, you may give and take on a lot of areas in your life, but you will never budge when it comes to your rights. Now it must be noted that we are talking about personal rights we claim for ourselves, not the rights that we fight to give to the weak and less fortunate.

These personal rights that inform many of our choices many times stand in stark comparison to the life of faith, which gives up all of its rights. Jesus explained this idea to His disciples as they expressed their need to do the things they believed were well within their rights. Take a look:

As they were traveling on the road someone said to Him,

"I will follow You wherever You go!"

Jesus told him, "Foxes have dens, and birds of the sky have nests, but the Son of Man has no place to lay His head." Then He said to another, "Follow Me."

"Lord," he said, "first let me go bury my father."

But He told him, "Let the dead bury their own dead, but you go and spread the news of the kingdom of God."

Another also said, "I will follow You, Lord, but first let me go and say good-bye to those at my house."

But Jesus said to him, "No one who puts his hand to the plow and looks back is fit for the kingdom of God." (Luke 9:57–62)

These disciples hearing and seeing Jesus face-to-face still fell back on the rights they believed should take precedence over following Him. The first guy would follow Jesus only after he buried his father. This Jewish law took priority over everything else, even his worship of Jesus. It was, after all, not just law but the right of a child to bury their parent. Jesus, however, suggested that the dead bury themselves, showing that giving up what the man felt was a right was actually the cost of discipleship.

The second man would follow only after he was allowed to go back home and say good-bye to his family. But this, Jesus objected to as well—showing that not even family ties take precedence over the life of faith.

When you begin to have a sense of your rights, you begin to pull away from Christ. Your rights demand your allegiance, and Jesus said that you cannot give allegiance to two different masters (see Matt. 6:24)—that would be dividing your heart and your will. When the two allegiances conflict, who wins? The longer you stand on your rights, the harder it is to choose Jesus in a stand-off.

So another cost of faith is the giving up of all your rights but one—the right to approach a holy God and glorify Him even though you are a sinner. This is your right given to you as a gift through Jesus' death on the cross. Glorifying God is the purpose for your existence, the reason God created you. When you stand on any other right than this, you open yourself up to doubt, worry, and fear. You open yourself up to disagreements with your God and a redefining of who God is. As you fight for your rights, you focus all of your energy on yourself rather than on God, and in so doing, there is a shift in your faith.

What Jesus is asking of you is nothing that He hasn't already done Himself. When He was about to be crucified, and His rights were being abused, "The high priest then stood up and said to Him, 'Don't You have an answer to what these men are testifying against You?' But Jesus kept silent" (Matt. 26:62–63). Though Jesus had the right to argue His case, He didn't stand on that right. That is because He was sure the will of the Father would be done. Jesus was content with that will, however hard it would be for Him, because it would bring His Father glory.

The World

All of this talk about the cost of ownership involves an understanding of this world and the next. As long as you continue to think highly of the things of this world, to judge things based on what the world considers good and useful, your faith will be in this world and will not venture beyond to the things of heaven. But as we saw in the very act of the crucifixion of Christ, our worldly thoughts on right and wrong don't apply. As Jesus Himself confirmed, "My kingdom is not of this world. . . . If My kingdom were of this world, My servants would fight, so that I wouldn't be handed over to the Jews. As it is, My kingdom does not have its origin here" (John 18:36). As long as you consider your origins to be this world, you will continue the fight that the world calls you to join. When the world is the filter for your life and your choices, the gospel of Jesus becomes watered down with other allegiances and loyalties, and the faith you find yourself with isn't faith in God but in His creation.

God's Word makes it clear that the cost of faith must be your love affair with the world.

> Do not love the world or the things that belong to
> the world. If anyone loves the world, love for the
> Father is not in him. For everything that belongs
> to the world—the lust of the flesh, the lust of the
> eyes, and the pride in one's lifestyle—is not from
> the Father, but is from the world. And the world
> with its lust is passing away, but the one who does
> God's will remains forever. (1 John 2:15–17)

When you love the world, you want what it offers; the temptation for fame, success, money, acceptance, all of them whisper, and sometimes shout at you, from every direction. It's tantalizing and promising. For a time you will believe its promises as you try to reconcile the world's plans with God's. And for a time you might succeed at that, thinking that they can both coexist peacefully. But God asks the question in James, "Don't you know that friendship with the world is hostility toward God? So whoever wants to be the world's friend becomes God's enemy" (James 4:4). That doesn't mean God wants you to hate people, nature, or any of His creation; it just means that preferring the thoughts of the world—the things the world covets, believes, or teaches—over the thoughts of God is hostility to God.

Let's break that idea down. Friendship involves agreement. When you hang out with a friend, it's because of what you have in common, what you like to do together. Friends share interests, ideas, beliefs, and convictions. Friends inform your decisions, give you advice, encourage you or discourage you, and that's why friendship with the world is a sin. In this reference to friendship, the world with all of its worldly, rather than spiritual, concerns pulls you away from God and even demands your allegiance to it over God. It advises you against Him and comforts you when He is seemingly unruly or harsh. **The world doesn't know God, and so their opinions on His actions toward you are always incorrect.**

But the world offers you some tantalizing treats, all of which promise to satisfy your soul. The world is tangible; it's loud and it never shuts up; it's ever pushing and ever pulling you in all different directions. It wants to meet your needs and it continually offers you instant gratification and future success. But this instant gratification affects eternal reward. As Jesus asks you in Matthew 16:26, "What will it benefit a man if he gains the whole world yet loses his life? Or what will a man give in exchange for his life?"

➡ **Hayley's World:** All of my life I believed I would be famous. I dreamt of it, worked for it, and was certain it was coming. After college I started to do a lot of performing, acting, and singing, and soon I was "discovered." A producer found me and wanted to produce my first album. I was excited beyond belief! I set myself to the hard work of making music and building an image that the world would love. Hair got done, wardrobe was selected, photo shoots took place, and the world was my oyster, until He showed up. One fateful night a boy I knew introduced me to the grace of God, and my life was forever changed. When I heard the amazing news that God still loved me even though I had messed up so much for so long, I was transformed.

Not long after that, a choice had to be made. My God or the world? Him or fame? I knew deep down in my soul it had to be done. I couldn't keep on pursuing the love of man and the love of God. The two were inconsistent. And so on a summer's evening in my old Volkswagen Bug, I asked God if I could trust Him and walk away from my dreams. Somehow I knew I could and that one day He would give me more than I had ever dreamed. At that point I stopped all my music, all my performing for the world, and gave it all to Him. And I never looked back. But true to form, God gave me more than I ever could have dreamt of. I now am doing what I love more than anything and getting up in front of thousands, talking to millions about the most important thing in the world: God's love. And I wouldn't change it for all the adoration of the world. Instead of going for my glory, I have gone for His, and He has given me the most incredible life in the world. ←

True faith in Christ means giving up your faith in the world. This isn't to say that you become disillusioned with people or your future, but that you consider yourself not of this world. Rather than a citizen of earth, you are a citizen of heaven (see Phil. 3:20), and so you are only an ambassador here, living to serve the King, and not yourself. Therefore, the best advice for you is not to get "involved in civilian life" but to live to please your commanding officer (see 2 Tim. 2:4). Don't let the world have your faith. It will not serve you and it will not save you. But when you give up your hope in the world and all its treasures—when you let it go and instead live only for the praises of God—then and only then will your faith save you.

It must be understood now, before you go any further, that what we are talking about is a radical change to your life. Up until now you have loved and been loved by the world. But once you pay the price of worldly adoration, the world will not be happy. That's why this is often the greatest and most feared cost. Because as Jesus says in John 15:19: "If you were of the world, the world would love you as its own. However, because you are not of the world, but I have chosen you out of it, the world hates you." **If the world doesn't hate you, then, according to this verse, He hasn't chosen you out of it.** Are you willing to be hated by the world? To be thought of as a freak? An idiot? A loser? If you are not, then you are still putting your faith in yourself and the world. But if God has given you the will to walk away from the stuff this world offers and even demands, then faith is yours, so grab it!

As you begin to give up the race to be your own god and instead turn your life over to the only true God, the world is going to be watching and laughing. Those who haven't surrendered find the very act of surrender to be sheer stupidity. They have no faith in God, so letting go of your life to Him is like jumping into the deep end of the pool and refusing to swim. And that's just how it might feel to you today. But trusting God isn't stupidity, but purpose. You weren't made to save yourself. You weren't made to struggle for control, to punish yourself, to fight for your rights, or to be deceived by the world. You were made for one purpose and one purpose only: to bring glory to God and enjoy Him forever. As you go from bringing glory to yourself through all of these things, His glory shines on you. And in that glory you find the freedom you've longed for, for so long, and the peace that has never been yours— peace that only comes through a reconciled relationship with Jesus Christ.

4

Owning Your Faith
Will Change You

People think that God is about forgiving and
getting as many people into heaven as He can. Wrong!
He is about transforming people.
— JAMES MACDONALD

The transformation of a human embryo is nothing short of miraculous. As soon as a baby is conceived, he is growing, forever changing, becoming different than he was yesterday. It's part of being alive. When you live, you grow. **At the point that you stop growing, you start dying.** It is impossible for a living thing to not grow. And all growth involves change. Change is the evidence of growth. A tree that is growing changes from season to season, growing leaves, shedding them, and growing them back again. Your body does the same thing. Your very cells are constantly growing and changing, regenerating and dying. The cells in your stomach change about every five days. The cells in your skin change every week. Living means changing, growing. The only person who isn't growing is decaying, dying.

But that's your physical life; what about the rest of you? Does your personality change like your cells? If you were born an introvert, do you stay one forever? Or is that something you can grow out of, like your baby teeth or your curly hair? The idea that you are who you are and you just have to learn to love it and others just have to learn to live with it is a popular one. A lot of people believe that whatever nature or nurture has instilled in them is what they are stuck with. So a person might be called dumb as a kid and think that's a life sentence. Or they might be prone to anger or shyness and believe that to be as natural to them as their physical traits of height and build and just as unchangeable. But in the life of faith, that's not the reality of the situation.

Faith signals a change, not only in your eternal destination but in your heart, your mind, and yes,

even in your personality. When you own your faith, those things that used to control you lose their power. The stuff that used to scare you is uneventful. Faith—true faith—changes you from the inside out. As we read in 2 Corinthians 5:17, "If anyone is in Christ, he is a new creation; old things have passed away, and look, new things have come." A new creation is a changed creation. In other words, just as your cells die off and are replaced by new ones, so the old self dies off and is replaced, only not by an exact replica but by a better, more improved version of you.

This new life is one that stands in stark contrast to your old life. In your old life you were controlled by sin, addicted, losing the battle, wandering and hopeless. Any gains you made, any ground you gained, came at the expense of other ground and with other losses. And the fight never seemed to stop. But in the new life, you are set free from the chains of sin and instead are purified and living in the light of truth (see Eph. 4:21–24) rather than the deceit of darkness. And that's why we can say these very important nine words: **if God isn't changing you, then He hasn't saved you.** Contact with God opens your eyes not only to your own failure and sin but to His greatness, power, and love, and in that comes His changing force on your very soul. When you truly see the love of God—His grace, His forgiveness, and His generosity—then you can no longer stay the same. Every day as the Holy Spirit renews your mind through His Word, you are changed.

When you remain unchanged by your faith, it is because your faith is more deeply rooted in self than in God. Self makes demands. Self wants to be heard, to be satisfied. And when you kowtow to yourself, when you answer to yourself, and when you live to serve yourself, your self is not up for debate. In other words, you will not discuss the idea of change because of the impact it will have on who you are. This kind of thinking—that who you are is the most important thing about you—is an enormous barrier to faith. Because as long as you think that you are too important to lose, that you are unique and special, and that you are just trying to be the best you, you can be sure that you will never be the you that God wants you to be.

So many times it's scary to think about the change that God wants in your life. What will He get rid of and what will He keep? The idea that someone outside of you decides ultimately who you are disagrees with all of the self-protection you've relied on your entire life. But how has this self-protection served you? Has it given you all that it promised it would? Is your life free from the control of things like anger, fear, bitterness, addiction, doubt, isolation, and worry? Are you living the life? Embracing everything, both good and bad, that comes your way, fearless in the face of failure? Or maybe you have a hunch that there is somehow more. When you find that life, no matter how hard you go at, isn't all that you sense it could be, then you've come to a good place. Until you can give up the hold you have on your self-life, you won't find the freedom and hope that God is waiting to give you.

A Change of Heart

Owning your faith will change you; that is a certainty. It will change what you love, what you do, how you look, what you believe, what you feel, and what you dream. There is no way to own your faith and not find yourself changing. Because you are not perfect and God is, the more you look at Him and love Him, the more you want less of you and more of Him. And **with that recognition of your own failure and weakness comes a willingness to be done with all the stuff in you that is inconsistent with Jesus in you.**

There is a conflict that flares up when you have Christ living in you alongside your sin. They are incompatible, and because of that you are left with a choice: **will you love the sin or the Savior?** When you choose to love the sin, you opt for a life without change. But when you choose to love the Savior, then change is unavoidable because the affection of your heart calls for a change of allegiances. As long as you look at your moral failure as anything less than sin, you will avoid change because calling sin a "struggle" or an "indulgence" fools yourself into thinking that keeping the sin will be less painful to your life than giving it up. In other words, **until the idea of change becomes less painful to you than the sin you are living in, change won't be an option.** For example, a person with an addiction is powerless to walk away from the addiction until keeping it becomes more painful than leaving it. Or to put it spiritually, for a lot of people the idea of turning themselves over to Christ sounds more painful than the addiction they live in, so they don't budge. But when you recognize the depth of your failure and the heights of His love and grace, the idea of holding on to your sin becomes more painful than letting it go, and that leads to change.

The Bible refers to this change as repentance. **Repentance is the act of changing your mind about God.** When you embraced your sin as either acceptable or as an inevitable struggle of life, then you rejected God by rejecting His thoughts on sin, by disagreeing with Him. **But when you own your faith, you also own your sin.**

And as you own up to the sin in your life, you are left with an incredible urge to be done with it, to repent. The *Tyndale Bible Dictionary* says this about repentance: *"It is inconsistent and unintelligible to suppose that anyone could believe in Christ yet not repent."*[1] When you repent, you stop what you are doing in order to do something else—in other words, you change. In this way owning your faith will change you. And not just once at the point of conversion, but daily.

Whenever you experience guilt, or the recognition of your sin, if the outcome isn't repentance, it's going to be death. Second Corinthians 7:10 explains it this way: "Godly grief produces a repentance not to be regretted and leading to salvation, but worldly grief produces death." In this verse, grief is synonymous with guilt. Godly guilt, the kind that signals a rejection of God, is good guilt because it gives you the desire to change—without it you wouldn't know you had done anything wrong. But worldly guilt, or bad guilt as we have already mentioned, produces death because it keeps you from the change of repentance that saves you from the death of your nearness with God. In other words, when you sin and ignore the guilt—or when you acknowledge the guilt but reject the forgiveness of God in favor of self-punishment or self-hate—your unwillingness to change, to agree with God and His forgiveness, serves to destroy you. It may be a slow, silent death, but it is a death all the same because it is a separation from God and, instead, union with the chains of sin.

We are all sinful as we read in 1 John 1:10, "If we say, 'We don't have any sin,' we make Him a liar, and His word is not in us." Since there isn't anyone who's perfect but Jesus, the change that comes from repentance is a never-ending thing. In fact, you could easily find the need to repent daily. At the very least, to reject your accidental sin in favor of God's love, and so to turn away from the allure of sin and its assault on your relationship with Him.

Repentance can be a dangerous thing to your self-life. That's because it accuses you of error, of failure, and that can translate into the accusation of being a "bad person." No one wants to think of themselves as bad. But "being bad" is no indictment on your salvation, or God's ability to love you, but rather evidence of God's truthfulness in His Word. If you could be good in your own power, then you don't need Jesus. As we read in Galatians 2:21, "If righteousness comes through the law, then Christ died for nothing." So not accepting the forgiveness afforded you by the blood of Christ is saying to Him, "Yeah, that whole cross thing . . . waste of time. Sorry to say it, but while it might be good for everyone else, it's just not good enough for me." Ouch. That doesn't sound so good when it's put that way, does it? We all have sinned and we all need forgiveness, and when you realize that that's why Jesus hung on the cross, you are met with the opportunity for change—change of heart and change of action, because to not change is to reject His perfect work on the cross.

Change is natural to the life of faith because repentance requires it and the cross provides for it. If you are not changing, then you are making the sin in your life acceptable to you, and therefore rejecting God and His Word. If you are afraid of repentance, then it might be because you are afraid of God's view of your sin, so let these words of Christ be an encouragement to you: "There will be more joy in heaven over one sinner who repents than over 99 righteous people who don't need repentance" (Luke 15:7). **God loves to hear about your sin.** He is eager to hear your confession and to lead you in your repentance. But you have to be willing to change. *The New American Commentary* on 1 John puts the idea of your sin into perspective with the statement that "you are not sinful because you sin, you sin because you are sinful."[2] Letting your sin designate you "bad" is a misunderstanding of your sin nature. You don't sin because you became bad but because you were born a sinner; it's your nature, so it comes as no surprise to God when you fail. But it comes as great joy when you agree with Him and repent from your sin.

What you love

What you love reveals as much about you as what you reject. Love points to allegiance, to sacrifice, and to worship. Love controls not only your heart and your emotions but also your actions. When you love someone, you will do anything for them. When you love something, you will do anything to protect it or to get it. But when you have faith in God, what you love changes. In fact, God commands it to change, as you can see in 1 John 2:15–17:

> Do not love the world or the things that belong to the world. If anyone loves the world, love for the Father is not in him. For everything that belongs to the world—the lust of the flesh, the lust of the eyes, and the pride in one's lifestyle—is not from the Father, but is from the world. And the world with its lust is passing away, but the one who does God's will remains forever.

Here you are told not to love the world. But what does that mean? What is the world and the things that belong to it? And how can you avoid loving them when you live with them? The answers to these questions are found in this same passage. Three things that belong to the world are listed here. **The first one is the lust of the flesh.** You might think this is just talking about sexual lust, but that's not what this verse means. Lust isn't a negative or positive term as it's used here; it's neutral. So it's not about lust in the way we use the word, with sexual stuff. But it's about the desires of the flesh that you give in to. In other words, **it's about loving something so much that you overdo it.** Like you love food so much that you overeat it. Or you love exercise so much that you build too much muscle or become dangerously thin. Overindulgence of your flesh in any area belongs to the world. A good way to think of lust here is the idea of using more than you need of anything. **When you overindulge in whatever it might be, then you are no longer loving God but yourself and your pleasure.** As Paul puts it in 1 Corinthians 6:12, "'Everything is permissible for me,' but not everything is helpful. 'Everything is permissible for me,' but I will not be brought under the control of anything." The world would have you overindulge your senses. Dive in and lose yourself in them. But God wants your senses tuned to Him and not to your own pleasure.

Changing what you love and what you indulge in is an essential change that comes supernaturally in your life as you grow in faith. **If you don't find yourself**

rejecting the call of your flesh for more, then you haven't yet believed God and His Word. But when you own your faith, you agree with God and reject the lust of your flesh in favor of your desire for God. And you call sin, sin.

The second thing that belongs to the world in this passage is **the lust of the eyes**. Like the lust of the flesh, this isn't all about sex. But it's **a craving for the stuff that you see.** Call it materialism or greed and you'd be right. When you see the things of this world and wish they were yours, your complaint against God starts. "Why don't I have that?" you ask. "I need that," you say. You accuse God of not providing for your needs. Then after complaints are vented, the job of fixing the situation gets under way. In this, you take life into your own hands as you manufacture the circumstances that will get you what your eyes long for. This might be for material things like cars, houses, jewels, etc. Or it might be for emotional things like fame, acceptance, or love. Whatever you have seen that you crave—what you set your heart on—betrays your love for the world. **Even if what you crave seems godly and good, when you lust for something you do not have (or have enough of), you experience envy or greed.** And envy and greed are desires for self-indulgence rather than faithfulness.

The lust of the eyes captures many an unsuspecting Christian soul. As your faith compels you to worship God, what you see around you distracts you and gets you back onto the subject of you. But when you truly own your faith, this lust starts to change as you see the things of this world, even the good things, as gifts in the hands of the Father rather than prizes you have to own. **Lusting for anything other than God is disaster and leads to a failure to embrace the change that God would have in your life.** But true contentment comes to you when you prefer God's will to your own.

Finally, **the pride of one's lifestyle,** also described as "bragging about yourself," is a symptom of being in love with the world over God. **When you talk about your stuff, your success, yourself, then you practice pride.** And this pride reveals how much the world means to you, because **at the root of the pride in yourself is the desire for others to see you in a good light and to love you.** When you want the approval of the world, you reject the approval of God. When man's thoughts on you matter more than the One who can save you, your love exposes your worldliness. In Galatians 1:10 the author asks, "Am I now trying to win the favor of people, or God? Or am I striving to please people? If I were still trying to please people, I would not be a slave of Christ." What's the answer you get when you ask yourself these questions? The answer will reveal to you your affection, and your faith. If you worship God only because you are trying to please people, then you aren't worshipping God but the people. And if you want the approval of man so much that you will reject God's and His love, then the love of God is not in you.

You cannot truly own your faith in Christ as long as there is a person between you and God. But loving God means getting face to face with Him and rejecting the pride you have in proving yourself to others. This should offer you freedom. Pleasing people is an unending task, and one that dooms you to failure. But pleasing God is easy when it's all that you desire. Not that you will be perfect, but that you will desire change as soon as you realize you have failed Him. In that desire for change you will find the freedom that comes with His forgiveness and His Son fulfilling the law for you.

As long as you put your hope in your own abilities and resources or in the beauty and reliability of the creation rather than the Creator, you will fail to own the faith that God is offering you.

What you feel

What you think about your feelings has a huge impact on how you feel. It goes like this: if you believe that your feelings are a good guide in life, than whatever you are feeling at any given time is very important to you. After all, it's an insight into your circumstances, a clue about your suffering and your success. **Believing that your feelings are reliable and beneficial when listened to will only serve to magnify those feelings.** So feel an eerie sense of doom and you are going to feed that doom when you deem it intelligent and worthy of response; you are going to focus on it, investigate it, and encourage it in your life. Having these sorts of thoughts about the validity of your feelings makes feelings a powerful force in your life. And since they are so volatile and fickle, your life can feel like a roller coaster, never staying in one place, always rising and falling, twisting and diving.

When you use your feelings as your guide, you allow them to not only tell you what to do but they tell you what not to do. And so feelings become the final say between you and your next action. In other words, they are the filter for your interpretation of the things that God has to say to you. But bet you wouldn't be surprised to know that when you own your faith, your feelings will change. Or maybe a better way to say it is, what you feel about your feelings will change.

Faith has a lot to say about your heart and the things it tells your head. For example, "The heart is more deceitful than anything else, and incurable—who can understand it?" (Jer. 17:9). Much of the time, your feelings are the reaction of your flesh, the part of you that is earthly and selfish. The flesh resists the Spirit, wars against it, and tries to gain control. The flesh wants what it wants and often makes very loud demands. And so the feelings you have of bitterness, hatred, lust, regret, worry, and emotions like them are centered in your flesh, not in God's Spirit. But the true believer is aware of this battle, and even though they might fail from time to time, they never give up the fight. And so when feelings scream something that goes against the Word of God, the Christian rejects their own feelings and stands on faith.

➡ **Hayley's Feelings on Faith:** Just out of college I dated this older man. He was a professional photographer and a smooth talker. So smooth that when my feelings for him were overflowing and I wanted an outlet for them, he was able to convince me of this little known fact (which he made up): "Why would God make sex if He didn't want you to do it?" That little justification took away my sense of right and wrong, and blurred the lines just enough for me to go too far with him. If I had truly owned my faith at the time, I wouldn't have been such a pushover. My feelings might still have been as strong, but I would have been able to say no to them and seen the twisting of the truth he so masterfully played on me. ←

So, when your feelings tell you to do something like "Just relax! Forget about God for the night and have some fun! After all, you deserve it; besides, you can just confess in the morning and it will all be okay," you are left with little chance to change. Change means saying no to your oh-so-tempting feelings, but staying the same means giving in because their voice is just too sweet. When your feelings talk, they often pretend to be something they are not, like God. It can be hard to tell the difference between your thoughts and God's voice, especially when you don't *really* recognize it. When you act on what you think is God's voice, it can be an honest mistake, but you can't do that anymore. We've pulled the cover off the truth that's been hiding and we are exposing it for you. Sorry for that! But let's strip it down some more. Here are some things that your feelings tend to say to you that are *not* the voice of God. So if you think them, or hear them, then you can quickly say a loud and resounding "No!" to them.

Feelings say things like:

- You deserve it!
- Just one more.

Own It

- You only live once!
- Did God really say _____?
- What can it hurt?
- Today it's going to be all about you.
- She/he started it and you gotta finish it!
- Nobody loves you.
- You are too weak to control yourself.
- If it feels good, do it!
- The end justifies the means.
- You are worthless.
- You can just ask God to forgive you after you're done.
- If you do this, you will feel so much better.
- Revenge is sweet.
- Do whatever it takes to get what you want.
- Second place is just first loser.
- You feel so bad you're gonna die.
- Being alone is the worst thing in the world.
- God can never forgive you.
- You're not good enough for God.
- You need to work harder at faith.

The more you say no to these lies and to your feelings and replace them with what Philippians 4:8 describes— "Whatever is true, whatever is honorable, whatever is just, whatever is pure, whatever is lovely, whatever is commendable—if there is any moral excellence and if there is any praise"—the more you find yourself living in the peace of God. When you see the result of rejecting your sinful feelings, it just makes you want to reject some more. As those bad feelings pop into your head again, you begin to want them gone. And so goes faith—God changes you more and more each day as He reveals to you the areas in your life where you have given your feelings too much control.

In all of this, change is made possible by God, who turns on the light in your life and shows you what you previously were blind to see. After all, we read in Isaiah that He is the one who blinded you—why shouldn't He then be the one who opens your eyes? "Such people do not comprehend and cannot understand, for He has shut their eyes so they cannot see, and their minds so they cannot understand" (Isa. 44:18). **At the point that God reveals Himself to you and shows you the sin in your life, He begins the changing process.** Once He's shown you the light, once you are taught by God, you cannot go back into darkness without feeling the sting of living a lie.

What you do

As what you love and how you feel changes, it's only natural then that what you do changes too. There is no way to change the first two things in your life without changing the third. If a person's actions aren't consistent with what they believe, then we call that person a hypo-crite. Their actions betray their heart and let the world see what they really love and how they really feel. But when the Holy Spirit reveals Himself to you, when He turns on the divine light, your actions follow, and they are changed.

If you've tried and failed to be good, you might think that obedience to God is impossible, and that is true, in your own power it is. No one, who isn't listening and liv-ing by the power of the Spirit, can obey God. They might act like they are, but their motive, if you could know it, would reveal that they are acting in the flesh, looking for the big payoff. And that's not faith; that's fake. When you turn your life over to God and have no designs on it, yourself or your actions, begin to follow His desires. And when that happens, the fruit of self-control infiltrates your life and overflows. It's not that you become a super-perfect human being at the point of salvation, but the process of change begins. Those things that God chooses to reveal to you start to slough off as the edges of your life are polished. Things you might never have even considered out-of-bounds to you suddenly look unacceptable. And not necessarily because they are sin, but just because the Spirit of God has shown you a better way.

➡ **Michael's Big Change:** The first Bible verse I ever memorized was when I was seventeen. It was 2 Corinthians 5:17: "Therefore, if anyone is in Christ, he is a new creation; old things have passed away, and look, new things have come." Even though I had committed this verse to memory, it didn't really change me. I didn't realize what "in Christ" meant. I thought it meant that I had said a magic prayer and vowed to be as good as I could, that Jesus was going to help me walk the tightrope of goodness that I couldn't walk myself. But it wasn't until over a decade later when I sat in a jail cell and opened up that old Gideon Bible that the verse supernaturally made sense. "In Christ." It wasn't my efforts but Christ's perfect life that made me good in God's sight. A totally new creation in His eyes. "In Christ" meant my life and everything surrounding it were new because Christ was now the filter; I was in Him and could see nothing without Him affecting my vision. That's when I learned that true change can't come from a sinner's heart, but only from a God who loves us and changes us in spite of our hearts. ⬅

If there are things in your life that you've tried to stop but have failed to get any control over, then it is because you haven't taken God at His Word when it says, "It is God who is working in you, enabling you both to desire and to work out His good purpose" (Phil. 2:13). As you turn your life over to God and own your faith, He works in you to do those things that He has purposed for you. And that's how change is such an integral part of the life of faith, because God is the great changer of persons. He never leaves you the same but is always helping you, guiding you, and teaching you to become more and more like His Son, more and more perfect through His Son. And it isn't by anything that you work hard at or struggle against, but it's His strength that transforms you. "For by one offering He has perfected forever those who are sanctified" (Heb. 10:14). You might not feel this perfection in your life, but that's because you have been focusing on the wrong thing. Take your eyes off of yourself and put them onto the Spirit that He has given you and you will see the change that you used to believe was unavailable to you. Being mindful of His Spirit and its power will set you free and move you more toward the perfection of Christ.

➡ **Hayley's Old Look:** When I first started going to church, I was driving limousines and living the life of the world. I can remember my best outfit, and the one I wore to church: a black lace miniskirt, the size of a large belt; stockings that came out just below it, attached to a garter belt; and a black vest with nothing underneath it. I was the epitome of trashy fashion. And I thought it was cute. I was completely oblivious. I dressed in order to be hot, to get attention, and to land me a man, not to please God. That never entered my mind. Then one day my friend Tina, who was discipling me for a month or so, told me she needed to talk to me about clothes. "You know that how you dress is sexy?" "Yep," I said. "If you've got it flaunt it, right?" I snickered and jabbed her with my elbow. She smiled and kindly said, "Well, not really." She then went on to explain to me how my body, and specifically my way of showing it off, could lead boys and men into temptation. As soon as she said it, I got it. I cried a bit for my complete ignorance of anything spiritual, but quickly went home and opened up my closet to clean it out. When the lights came on in my fashion life, a change had to be made. And because I loved God so much and wanted to please Him, I was happy to rethink my clothing choices and change my life. ◄

How you look

Change is a part of every area of life, even the visual. Some might say *especially* the visual. The world says,

"This is your life, you can look however you want, and they have to get over it." But God says to consider others more important than yourself (see Phil. 2:3). And when you hear that and you want to do it, your life is going to change. Like Hayley, as you understand how ignorant you were before you knew anything, you want to act on your newfound knowledge. And so faith leads to a change in your look. Whether it's no longer dressing to catch the eye of the opposite sex or making decisions against getting obscene tattoos, change affects your wardrobe, your accessories, and your look.

The most obvious area that is affected by your love for God is your sexy parts. When you read that Jesus says it would be better to be thrown into the lake with a millstone tied around your neck than to lead another believer to sin, you have to take into account your role in the temptation of others (see Mark 9:42). That means if you are a girl showing off your nice chest, midriff, or lower back, then you are playing with fire. If you're a guy and you're constantly taking off your shirt to show off your abs or how ripped you are, you too are playing with fire. Wanting to get attention for yourself rather than focusing it all on God is a dangerous proposition. But wanting Him to be the star, the most important person in the room, means being modest and refusing to demand all the attention. And the same goes for your look when it comes to the way you command a room, steal the limelight, or in any way draw all eyes to you. **Wanting the world to look at you and applaud reveals a love of self that pushes out any love for God** and makes you the idol others should worship. But pointing all eyes up, driving their eyes away from you and to their Savior, is just the change that will restore your relationship with God and set you free from needing the approval of man.

What you dream

How you see yourself and your future affects how you live. And especially how you dream. If you see yourself becoming the best athlete in your sport, then you may dream of the fame that comes with that. If you see yourself having the perfect family, with the picket fence, the hybrid car parked in the driveway, and the 2.5 kids, then your dream will drive you to acquire all that you desire. That's just what our dreams do—they guide us, steer us, and control our choices and our faith. That's because we tend to put our faith in whatever will get us where we want to go—be it a fitness routine, a dating technique, or a self-help guru—if something or someone promises you all you've dreamt of, your allegiance can easily follow. Dreams propel you through life. But **once you give your**

life fully to Christ, your dreams change. That's because your dreams used to be all about you and your worldly goals. But when you see how much more important He is, your dreams become irrelevant unless they are to see Him glorified more. As you focus on Him, your dreams that used to consume you become a distant memory, and your only goal is a daily one of being with Him and spending all your energy on Him.

If God hasn't changed your dreams, then you probably don't trust Him with them. You're afraid that He will take everything you dream away; He won't. But He will most definitely breathe into them and change them to serve not only Himself but you as well. For example, the guy who dreams of being a doctor and living the good life with a house in the hills and a yacht on the water, once he gives his life to Christ, might still dream of a life of medicine but the rest of the dream may change. He may now want to heal the poorest people with the least to give him in return. He may want to travel to distant lands and devote his life, not to the accumulation of stuff, but to the service of his God.

See, when you own your faith, **God owns your dreams,** and that means that everything you dream will fall through the filter of His glory and not your own. Your dreams will change because, truth be told, each of us, before surrendering our lives to God, lived only for ourselves. Our motives in dreaming are to make ourselves feel better, even if we are philanthropic; it is for the feeling we get when we do good. But God changes the subject to Himself, and suddenly your dreams become reordered. **If God hasn't reordered your dreams, then you have not turned yourself over to Him.**

➡ **Michael's Worst Nightmare:** Growing up, my parents were a lot older than my friends' parents; my dad was retired by the time I was a senior in high school. That meant he didn't have a lot of energy or youthfulness to share with me, didn't throw the ball around, didn't wrestle, stuff like that. He was a good dad, a wise dad, but I vowed to myself that I would marry young and be the kind of dad I wished I had. So I pursued this well-intentioned but self-centered dream through a number of relationships, desperately wanting multiple children of my own but each time ending in heartache for me and the woman I had pursued. It wasn't until after my jailhouse conversion that I gave up my dream to God and said, "I'm over thirty, I'm terrible at this. I want to live for You. I'm not dating anyone unless they drive me closer to You." I had released my dream of kids and even getting married. I met

Hayley a year later. We have an amazing daughter. She has a dad older than her friends. My life is a dream come true. ◄

Hopefully we've persuaded you that **if God isn't changing you, He hasn't saved you.** And hopefully you want the change to start, rather than fearing it. One of the things we often ask of people is this: **If you keep doing what you are doing, you'll keep getting what you've got.** Is that enough? If your answer is no, then change must come. Because to keep doing what you are doing but to expect change is the definition of insanity. So stop the insanity and consider the possibility of the changes of faith that take you from renter to owner and from lost to saved.

C. S. Lewis once said, *"We all want progress, but if you're on the wrong road, progress means doing an about-turn and walking back to the right road; in that case, the man who turns back soonest is the most progressive."* Don't be afraid to turn back. The wrong road won't end where it promises, and continuing to believe it will only prolongs the pain and delays the freedom. **If your life remains unchanged by God's grace, you don't really understand it. You might believe in God but you don't get the serious-ness of staying the same and what that says about your**

rejection of Christ's work on the cross. Don't let your increasing knowledge of God and His Word be the end of the experience for you, but allow it to change your life (see James 1:22–25). That is, after all, the goal of salvation, not just your ticket to heaven, but your changing from the old you to the new one. Do you really want to change, or do you just not want to get caught?

Notes

1. Walter A. Elwell and Philip Wesley Comfort, *Tyndale Bible Dictionary*, Tyndale reference library (Wheaton, IL: Tyndale House Publishers, 2001), 1119.

2. Daniel L. Akin, *1, 2, 3 John, The New American Commentary,* vol. 38 (Nashville: Broadman & Holman Publishers, 2001), 110.

5

Owning Your Faith Will Complete You

Heaven is not here, it's there. If we were given all we wanted here, our hearts would settle for this world rather than the next. God is forever luring us up and away from this one, wooing us to Himself and His still invisible Kingdom, where we will certainly find what we so keenly long for.
—ELISABETH ELLIOT

In the 1996 film *Jerry McGuire*, single mom Dorothy Boyd is recovering from the painful breakup she has just gone through with her former boss Jerry McGuire. Jerry had chosen his career over her and walked out on her. But as all good leading men do, this one had a change of heart. Yet when he comes traipsing back into her house, she isn't expecting the words that come out of his mouth. He explains how much he loves her, and while many might not be buying it, as soon as he says three now-famous words, there isn't one person in the room or watching in the theater who doesn't believe him. Jerry looks at Dorothy and says, as only actor Tom Cruise can, "You complete me." As soon as Dorothy and her friends hear it, they are all melting into the floor. And every woman in the audience is thinking about how great it would feel to hear those same words.

Deep down we all know the pain of being incomplete, and we desperately want to find the one who will fit into our lives like a hand in a glove, who will complete us. And likewise, the notion that someone confesses that you are their completion, says that life without you is undone, unfinished, half of what it could be, is grounds for rejoicing. Like Adam in the garden, we know that when the one for us comes along, we have found the other half of us, and in that we feel complete.

You complete me

The feeling of being incomplete can plague you and leave you feeling discontent, empty, broken, and lamenting your meaningless life. But **though finding someone to complete you is thoroughly romantic and dreamy, it is at its core flawed.** The flaw isn't in your assessment of need but in the parameters of your search. You do need someone to complete you, but believing that someone is another human being puts a responsibility and a strain on the person that they are not able to bear. And so when they fail to be all that you need—and they will fail—when they deceive you, hurt you, or leave you, your life goes from complete to a complete mess in a matter of minutes. When the person you determine will make you whole is gone, you are left broken and more incomplete than before your alleged completion.

So while Hollywood would love to get you to believe in the life-fulfilling power of the perfect relationship and the fantasy that true love is all you need to be perfectly complete, the truth is that another human being was never meant to be your salvation from the discontentment, pain, and loneliness of life.

I complete me

But maybe you don't put your hope in another human being because you've figured out you can do it all on your own. You don't need anyone in order to be complete. **This idea of completion is also flawed because it assumes**

that you were made for isolation, for a solitary life of self-sufficiency. It makes a life lived on its own a masterpiece that doesn't need anybody else, not even the artist. That's like a partially finished canvas saying, "I'm all I need to hang on the walls of the best museums in the world. I am a beauty in my own right." The canvas doesn't even see how it needs the artist and his brushes to complete it and make it what it was created to be. The truth is we all are incomplete and in need of something that we can neither generate on our own nor find in the creation.

As long as you are incomplete you are divided, half of you being or loving one thing and the other half of you being or loving another. With this division comes indecision—the inability to choose who you are or who you want to be. With indecision, the nagging feeling of being completely incomplete increases. This happens a lot in the misunderstood life of faith when you base your faith on what you've inherited or pretend to have. When your faith is for show and not really your own, then rather than being complete, you are living a divided life. Your mind goes back and forth between two opposing beliefs, and this indecision is tiring, if not destructive.

As long as your heart is divided, so is your mind, and the Bible says that a divided mind makes you unstable in all you do (see James 1:8). And that makes sense, right?

Because as long as your heart isn't committed to one direction, it will continue to pull you back and forth, up and down, causing you some heart instability, uncertainty, doubt, and even fear and worry. **But once you make a decision, your heart breathes a sigh of relief, and in that you find some comfort.** But the decision you have to make is whom will you serve? Yourself, another, or God?

The truth is that your heart was meant to be obsessed with love, not divided in love. It was meant to be given fully to the One and to One only, and that One, in case you haven't guessed it yet, is God. Your life will be incomplete, no matter who or what promises to complete you, as long as your heart is divided 50/50 or even 90/10. A divided heart serves no one. So to divide your quest for completion between God and man, even self, is a recipe for failure.

➡ **He Completes Me:** Most of my BC (before Christ) life I felt incomplete. I was divided so much between the love I felt for God and the doubt I had about His reliability that I played both sides and claimed faith while living in doubt. During that time I can remember feeling isolated even while in a group. I explained it as life in a bubble. I always felt like I was able to see and hear others, but because of the invisible bubble that surrounded me, I could not connect with them. Worse yet, I could not connect with God, but felt all alone—empty and sickened by everything I had heard would heal me. So in relationships with guys, I felt yucky and dirty, even though the relationship was what I wanted. In work, I felt extreme boredom and anxiety. And in life, I was fearful of everything. My bubble kept me feeling incomplete. But once I understood the power of God's love for me and His never-ending grace, the bubble popped, and suddenly life looked totally different. Rather than searching in the arms of another or in the glory of stardom for what I was lacking and being disappointed, I looked in the eyes of the Father and found Him saying, "I complete you."—**Hayley** ◀

Don't believe it? Then just take a look at the most successful people in the world and see the power of the undivided heart. Success in anything requires you give it your all—110 percent, as some like to say. It's no surprise that in order to succeed well at something you have to be present, you have to be devoted, obsessed even. So it should come as no shock to you that to be successful in loving God, you must love Him with all your heart, soul, and mind—100 percent of it (see Matt. 22:37). **Why do you feel incomplete?** Why do you search for completion in love or in success? **Because you were made to be complete—you are unfinished.** Looking for completion by giving any of your heart, soul, or mind designed for Him, to another, leads to human malfunction—the human serving in a capacity it was never designed to serve, the completer of your soul.

It would do well to mention here that this doesn't mean you cannot love another human being, but it means that **until you love God with all of your heart—something that only Christ can do through you—you will just love others with the selfish motive of needing them to complete you.** Love is selfless, not looking for the object of its love to do something for it, but loving without care for your needs. If you love someone based on your *need* for them, you do not fully love them, because loving others should never be about your needs. The two greatest commandments according to Jesus are to love God with all your heart, soul, and mind, and to love your neighbor as yourself. If you love God with 100 percent of your heart, then what percentage is left for your neighbor? None, unless loving God involves loving others as well. In this case, loving God must always be the foundation for loving others, and that is how we know that love is selfless, because there is no self in this equation.

The Narrow Road

The first step toward completion, then, is decision. Indecision is uncomfortable. It leaves you hanging, unstable, and easily toppled over and even controlled. The reason you remain in indecision is because you are ultimately afraid of making the wrong choice. And somehow not making a choice feels like safety. But the truth is, not making a choice *is* making a choice. It's choosing to avoid the fear of the narrow road with its small gate that must be entered in order to walk the path of faith. As Jesus explained, "Small is the gate and narrow the road that leads to life, and only a few find it" (Matt. 7:14 NIV). This narrow road can only be reached when you stop faltering, swaying, and bending back and forth between faith and unbelief.

As long as you hedge your bets by having a backup plan, you will never truly enter the road or own your faith. Up until now you may have believed that you had entered the faith. That you had committed and walked through the small gate. But as long as it has cost you nothing and changed you little, then perhaps you have only deceived yourself into believing that you have walked the road at all. That would be a helpful notion to consider, because that would mean that God wasn't a liar or a failure in your life. You just didn't truly commit yourself to the narrow road, but kept out a part of you for your own protection, use, or plans. In that case, there still remains to be seen the true power of God working in the life of a soul who gives 100 percent of their life to a God who will reward that act with His power and presence in a way that is rarely experienced. In order to enter the narrow gate, you must be stripped of your self-life and live only for Him and Him alone, with no excess baggage of self.

Completely Healed

When you live, you get hurt; it's a part of life. There is no way to escape the cuts, scrapes, and even gouges of living on planet Earth. The longer you live, the more wounded you can become. These wounds contribute to your sense of brokenness or incompleteness. The sensation of pain, loss, grief, and even struggle can leave a gaping hole in your heart that yearns to be filled. So as you search for the perfect person or thing to complete you, you are subconsciously looking for healing. The fears, doubts, worries, pain, and even dreams of your life look for answers in the stuff of this world, whether it's the creation or the creation's creation, their medicating benefit is the ultimate goal of a life that longs to be complete.

But medicating to feel complete just treats the symptoms rather than the cause. **Whether you are looking for the one person or the one drug to stop the pain, you are ultimately looking for a numbing agent rather than a healing one.** But there is an answer to all of this wound stuff, and that is in the one place you've probably looked but never fully considered to treat your wounds—the cross. On the cross the Savior was wounded, and His wounds became the balm for yours. As we see in Isaiah 53:5, "He was pierced because of our transgressions, crushed because of our iniquities; punishment for our peace was on Him, and *we are healed by His wounds*" (emphasis added).

As long as your wounds are more important than His, they will remain gaping and foul. They will sting and ooze discontentment and fear, and they won't be healed, only numbed. But once you see that His wounds took away your pain, that they have the power to heal your wounds in an instant, all you have to do is look away from yours and onto His and you will find complete healing. Your wounds suffer from your focus. When your focus is on your unattended to or neglected needs, pain, dreams, or hopes, then you are emotionally picking the scabs of your life and not allowing healing to take place. But **once you take your eyes off your wounds and put them onto**

His, you give your scabs the space to heal. Your heart is no longer broken, but whole and complete, and with that comes the release of your doubt, fear, and worry over future woundedness, because you are certain that His wounds are enough to cover even those. Only then can your self-protective urges find rest from your incessant emotional itching.

➡ As long as all of your attention is wrapped up in your own wounds, all your attention is put on yourself. But owning your faith means turning your attention away from yourself and onto God and God alone. Then and only then will you be completely healed, no matter how much the suffering lessens or increases. ⬅

Completely Protected

This idea of protection walks right alongside your thoughts on wounds as a guide, saving you from future harm and guarding your heart. When you yearn for something or someone to complete you, you yearn for a life of protection from the pains of your incomplete life. Imagine a life where your heart was completely protected, where it was bulletproof, and nothing could gut it again. When your heart is safe in the hands of the one who loves you the most, you feel complete. And you know this more than you know anything. Your heart must be protected, and in an attempt to do that, you have created all kinds of barriers, plans, and schemes.

You are not wrong in wanting to protect your heart; after all, the Bible warns you to "guard your heart above all else, for it is the source of life" (Prov. 4:23). The safest place for your heart is in the hands of one who loves you perfectly. But how do you put your heart into the hands of another? How do you ever truly protect your heart? The answer to this question is that you put your heart where you put your thoughts, desires, and needs. In other words, **when you give someone your heart, you give them your worship.** You adore them; you think about them all the time; you praise them; you give them thanks for all that they do for you; you believe in them; and you rest in the fact that they will never hurt you and never leave you. And that's why giving your heart to someone is so dangerous, because they have the ability to destroy you. You have basically given them the reins of your life.

God has an answer for this dilemma. When you surrender your heart to Him—when you give Him all your adoration, worship, thoughts, praise, thanks, and you trust Him to never leave you or forsake you—your heart is in His hands. In the hands of the perfect One, you are safe no matter what happens, no matter who you love, who rejects you, fails you, or in any way tries to hurt you, because your heart is encased in His perfect, powerful, and good embrace. With Him holding you and loving you, you can be sure that nothing reaches you unless it first gets through Him. And if He lets it through to you, then it must be for your good, because that is all that He ever allows. **So perfect is His love that to allow anything that was not for your ultimate good into your life goes completely against His nature.** Putting all of your faith in God rather than in man allows you to then truly love mankind without reserve or fear and without worrying about yourself in any way. This kind of faith allows missionaries to walk in confidence among cannibals, human traffickers, warlords, and persecutors. In this you can truly love, and in this you truly are safe from all that you used to fear.

➡ "Anyone who sees God's fingerprints on everything in the world, including insult and injury, cannot be destroyed and cannot harbor or nurse wounds at the hands of man, because they know that God's hand is far greater and His will far more important and powerful than the hands, the wills, and the power of man."—*The Fruitful Wife,* Hayley DiMarco ⬅

Completely Content

Another thing that you long for when you sense your emptiness is a sense of contentment. As long as you look around and see lack in your life, you will be discontent and incomplete. You know inherently that when you find the one who completes you that you will be happy, you will be content no matter if you live in a castle or a bamboo hut; being with the one you love will be all that you need. You know where this is going, so let's not beat around the bush. Any time you look for contentment in the world, in your surroundings, your relationships, or your experiences, you are looking for a cheap imitation of contentment, a whitewash on your rusted-out life that will one day melt off due to exposure to the elements. But when you come to the point of surrendering, not only your life but the requirements for that life to the One who provides everything that you need, then you will learn the secret of contentment in any and all situations.

The power of discontentment to feed the feelings of incompleteness in your life is nothing short of monumental. **The more you look at your life and bemoan your lack rather than your abundance, the more the hole in your life opens up.** Discontentment complains against God that He hasn't provided like a good Father should. It looks at the temperature of the room, the clouds in the sky, the size of a paycheck and says, "I deserve better." Discontentment speaks to the sense that life isn't going the way it should be going. But the life of faith—true faith that is unshakable—puts all the decision-making power into the hands of God, and in that bold move, faith rests on the idea that all is as it should be when God is in control.

We learn in Romans 8:28 that "all things work together for the good of those who love God: those who are called according to His purpose." When your faith is dead set on trusting God, on believing in His sovereignty in every area of your life, then contentment comes from trusting that no matter if it is adversity or good, they are both meant for your perfection.

As Paul learned and shared in his book to the Philippians, we can be content in all circumstances because whether we are full and happy or starving and sick, we can say, "I am able to do all things through Him who strengthens me" (Phil. 4:13). **When you own your faith, it completes you by giving you the certainty that there are no second causes in your life, but only one God through whom all must pass to get to you.**

➡ **Michael's Minimum Wage Contentment:**
I prayed the sinner's prayer when I was at a camp in high school. But I didn't learn the truth about

contentment until many years later when everything was stripped away from me. After making some really stupid decisions, I found myself in a jail cell telling God I was done doing life my way. At that point I walked away from my pretend faith and started to own it. Of course, the consequences for my actions weren't removed. I still had to live with the fact that I lost my job and most of my friends. I had to learn to live on $35 a month for food. And in those days of having nothing but my faith in God to guide me, I found the secret to contentment. Before, I had thought it was about feeling good about my life. But that was a lie; contentment is about knowing that God has you just where you are for a reason. As I did odd jobs in exchange for a room at a buddy's house, I applied for some really low-paying jobs and candidly talked about how I had stolen money from my previous job to gamble with. God honored my honesty, and I got a job with a great Christian company that believed in second chances and was promoted multiple times. But most of all God honored my obedience in His gift of a new life. ◄

Completely Fulfilled

Another thing that is promised by true love, money, fame, or success in whatever you pursue is fulfillment. When you are complete, you are fulfilled. Your life is filled with all the good stuff that you naturally long for—love, joy, peace, and even self-control—and you are satisfied. When you are complete, your life makes sense; it enlarges rather than shrinks. It is full, whole, one piece rather than fragmented and jagged. Ultimately we all just want to be happy. We believe that happiness comes from the things that we surround ourselves with. And while that is true, happiness is the result of the good stuff in your life; however, when the good stuff goes bad, happiness flies out the door. And often love does the same thing when human frailty and sin enters the picture. None of the virtues of life, none of the goodness seems to stick around when things get rough. Instead you are left with the emptiness of hate, sadness, strife, and a lack of self-control. The opposite things flood your life when circumstances shift from good to bad. But when your eyes are not on the circumstances that surround you but on the God you worship, things go differently.

If having faith hasn't meant fulfillment for you, but you have been looking for something more, then it's only because you haven't fully understood what true faith in

Christ is. **When you believe God, you don't just believe in His existence, but you believe *in* Him as the source of your fulfillment.** And we know that from the words found in Galatians 5:22–23, which describes the fruit of believing in God and allowing His Spirit to animate your life. Called "the fruit of the Spirit," it is a representation of complete fulfillment. This fruit is described as the fruit of love, joy, peace, patience, kindness, goodness, faithfulness, gentleness, and self-control. It describes a life of fulfillment. But not because of getting whatever you want, whenever you want it. Not because of perfect circumstances, but because of the fact that your life is no longer your own, you have given it all over to the life of the Spirit of God that lives inside of you. When you learn about His Spirit, when you see what He does, what He loves and what He hates, your eyes start to focus on the only thing in your life that can truly fulfill you. As you start to make your decisions based on His Spirit rather than your own, these fruits fulfill not only your life but the lives of those you share it with.

The fruit of the Spirit isn't reliant on circumstances. No matter what anybody else ever does to you or whatever else happens to you, you can still experience and exhibit all of this fulfilling fruit in your life, thus living a life that is completely fulfilled in all situations.

Completely Meant to Be

When we were single, we always wondered *How do you know when you've found the one?* And everyone who was married always said in their knowing sing-songy voice, "You'll just know . . ." And so for years we went through relationship after relationship looking for "the one." We were sure that once we laid eyes on them we would instinctually know it was meant to be. Every good love story has this element to it, doesn't it? This idea of "meant to be" is not only exciting but also romantic. It gives us a sense of purpose, a sense of destiny, and in that it gives our life meaning, especially all of the hard stuff—or as Rascal Flatts so eloquently thanks God for, "the broken road that led me straight to you." Until you find that person whom you were meant for, that job that was made just for you, or even the perfect car or house, you can feel incomplete, just longing for that meant-to-be thing to finish you.

When you think about your "meant to be" as something that is ordained—predestined to be yours—you should be really looking back instead of forward. Back to your creation, to the time when your fate was decided, when your way was laid and you were designed for a purpose. **There is, after all, no "meant to be" without someone who meant it, right?** And that's the place you have to start if you want to find your purpose in this world. To think that your purpose is simply to find the one or two important things you were meant to do or people you were meant to belong to is to limit your purpose. God does ordain your path, as we see in Proverbs 16:9: "A man's heart plans his way, but the LORD determines his steps." He doesn't just get involved when it has to do with the big things, like who you will marry or what job you will take. No, His involvement in your life reaches down to every aspect of it. In His divine will, He determines your purpose, your plan, the shape of your very life—just the way a potter decides what will become of his lump of clay (see Jer. 18:6).

In order to find your purpose in this world, you must look not to the faith of your parents or the faith you pretend to have but to God and your faith in His divine will. If you can believe that His hands are at work in all areas of your life, then you will never be alone, never left out in the cold, never without purpose. See, God's designed you for a purpose, and that purpose is to bring Him glory, for you to enjoy Him, to show Him to the rest of the world through them seeing the evidence of Him in your life. **God's purpose is to act in your life in a way that makes Him look good.** So even when things get bad, and I mean really bad, God can still get glory from your life when you reject what the world fears, worries about, or hates. Instead, you can trust God that His purpose for you will never go undone as long as you keep your eyes on Him and your heart in His hands.

In this way of thinking there is a very good way to determine if something or someone is meant to be. **If it amplifies the glory you can give to God, then it is meant to be. If whatever you are looking at for your life draws attention away from Him and onto you or onto something or someone else, then you can be sure it is not His best for you.** So if you are an artist who was meant to sing and you determine that you will do whatever it takes to make to be famous, then you run the risk of drawing attention away from God and onto your looks, your talent, or your drive. If you are going after any dream with the idea of what it will give you, do for you, or help you to become, then your faith isn't truly in God but in your dream.

When you own your faith, your life finds its meaning even in the mundane parts of life as you live it for Him and Him only. **Everything that happens to you is a part of your sanctification**—your change from moment to moment leading toward the perfection that will be yours when you enter eternity. If you feel incomplete because you don't know your purpose in this world, then embrace completeness when you agree that your purpose isn't anything less than the glory of God being seen in your daily life. "Therefore, whether you eat or drink, or whatever you do, do everything for God's glory" (1 Cor. 10:31).

It Is Finished

While on the cross, Jesus looked up to heaven and said the forever-remembered words, "It is finished." This was His cry of completion. Everything He was sent to do was complete at that moment. Every command and every prophecy was fulfilled, and it was done. It was done, not just for one man but also for the entire human race. This cry of completion accomplished the complete act of forgiveness and justification (see Rom. 3:24) for all who believe. That means that all the striving we live under, all the fear, all the work we feel compelled to finish before we can be complete is all for nothing, because Christ has already finished our work for us. **When your faith belongs to this world, when you get it from your parents or from your sense of fear, you know something is missing.** You can't put your finger on it, so you blame it on God, His absence, or even His nonexistence. But when your faith belongs to you—when you own it—then His act on the cross is all you need in order to be complete. It was, after all, His ultimate gift that provided all that you needed in order to have access to the giver of not only life but of hope, joy, peace, joy, and everything that is good in this world.

You can become complete today by simply making God the star of your life and bowing out of the role yourself. As you turn your back on your plans and fears and turn your face to His good and perfect will, then nothing can ever again break you or destroy you. Nothing that others intend to destroy you will be able to because God wills your salvation and not destruction. The desire that you have to rest in the arms of another human being in order to find your fulfillment will never truly satisfy you until your fulfillment is found in God Himself. He will then give you the joy of a relationship that goes down to the very heart of things—that bonds you not only physically but spiritually at a soul level. So turn your completion over to the only one who can truly affect it and be set free from the cares of this world. In Him you will be complete when you own your faith.

Owning Your Faith Will Free You

Do you want to be free from the bondage to sin? Would you like to grow in grace in general and grow in grace in particular? If you would, the way is plain. Ask God for more faith. Beg of him morning, and noon and night, while you walk, while you sit, when you lie down and when you rise up; beg him to simply impress divine things more deeply onto your heart, to give you more and more of the substance of things hoped for and of the evidence of things not seen.

—E. M. BOUNDS

In a room, there are only two doors. One is marked freedom, and the other is marked slavery. You go for the

one marked freedom because of what its name implies—
the ability to act without any kind of restraint or guilt.
And as you walk through, you find all kinds of tantalizing treats you are free to enjoy. In freedom there are no
demands, no worries, no chains. You can run free and
enjoy whatever you want to enjoy. And so you dig in.
And what you dig into is A-M-A-Z-I-N-G! So you keep
digging. And digging. Wow, freedom rocks! But then
you need to rest, so you sit down for a breather. But that
stuff was so great, how can a person rest? So you dig back
in. And over time you find it harder and harder to stop.
Pretty soon you are addicted, obsessed, or in some way
consumed. You aren't sure how it went from freedom to
bondage, but it did. And now the thing that allowed you
to let loose and dig in has chained you down and won't
let you go.

**Every addiction in your life at one point offered
freedom; that's how you got addicted. Freedom is the
calling card of slavery.** As long as you think that you are
free to do whatever you want, whenever you want, you
are blinded to the chains that clink around your feet and
hands. Think about it for a minute. Freedom to do whatever you want whenever you want feeds your appetites and
gives your desires free reign. And when they get it, they
take it. In other words, as you let loose and give yourself

permission to do something that you love, the mere fact that you love it, coupled with your stand on freedom, leads to overindulgence. And overindulgence develops addiction. When something is so great and so free, you have no reason to stop. And that's when you become addicted. It's simple really: desire plus freedom equals slavery.

Many would argue that freedom plus desire equals complete freedom, but check yourself and see if the things you have indulged in for your pleasure haven't led to a feeling of being out of control. For example, you might have given yourself sexual freedom, and then with each new act found it not to be enough and needed to go further. Or you may have given yourself the freedom to say whatever you are feeling, and now find that you can't control your anger with people. **At whatever point that you are out of control, you are a slave to whatever controls you.**

Freedom is the doorway to slavery. As long as you see freedom as the opportunity for you to do whatever you want whenever you want, you will obey your desires. Since you are a slave to whoever you obey, you become a slave to the stuff that feeds those desires. But maybe you think you have no desires that rule your behavior. Maybe you feel truly free. Then ask yourself this: "What compels me? What are my goals? What makes me do what I do?" Is there something that you can't live without? Without doing, without eating, without thinking? Do you wish you could control your tongue, your mind, your body? Are you perfect and able to stay clear of emotional turmoil, resentment, bitterness, hatred, vengeance, doubt, fear, worry, obsession? If you can say yes—you have total self-control and only do exactly what you want at exactly the right time—then think a little harder. **Because the truth is that there is no one who is free.** We are all in bondage to our very nature. The flesh that contains you is bound in the chains of sin. If that weren't so, then you would be unlike every other human being in the world, able to do whatever you want, whenever you want it, without control from either your own desires that battle against your will or from others.

If you don't see your chains, then you just haven't thoughtfully considered your condition. Singer songwriter Bob Dylan once rightly said, "No one is free. Even the birds are chained to the sky." Limited by their instinct, birds must live forever in the same region, not free to go wherever they will. And in the same way, what you have considered freedom all your life has actually been the doorway to bondage. So consider now your bondage. Consider the things that you know control you—things you wish you could stop, that make you emotionally weak, vulnerable, or sick. What things do you wish you could change? As long as you fail to own your faith, something or someone else will own you. Since owning your faith sets you free from the control of all the things of this world, you can rightly conclude that it puts you in slavery to the object of your faith. Now don't freak out. Remember, you cannot be free, so you have to choose who you will obey—your passions and desires that lead to bondage or your God who offers you freedom from the eternal consequences of and who gives rest, peace, joy, hope, love, and self-control.

And that's the thing: God offers freedom from slavery to the stuff that controls you, as you can see in Romans 6:20–22, "When you were slaves to sin, you were free from the control of righteousness. What benefit did you reap at that time from the things you are now ashamed of? Those things result in death! But now that you have been set free from sin and have become slaves to God, the benefit you reap leads to holiness, and the result is eternal life" (NIV). **Slave to sin or slave to righteousness, those are the options.** If it isn't one, it will be the other. And while sin satisfies in the moment, the price paid will not only be your life, but your happiness, your health, your self-respect, your peace, and your will.

"It is for freedom that Christ has set us free. Stand firm, then, and do not let yourselves be burdened again by a yoke of slavery" (Gal. 5:1 NIV). If the slavery to your supposed freedom controls you, then you can let Jesus set you free by simply owning your faith, owning His act of selflessness that sets you free from the power of sin.

Freedom

The freedom the world promised you was a lie; it was the doorway to slavery. But the freedom offered by Christ is true freedom; after all we read, "If the Son sets you free, you really will be free" (John 8:36). So what is this freedom? And how does owning your faith set you free? **The freedom that Christ gives you is freedom from the control of your flesh.** Your flesh is the root of all your problems because it holds your sinful nature. In your flesh is all that wars against God. Your flesh serves itself and not God, and so when your flesh sees something it wants, it goes for it without regard for safety, goodness, healthiness, or righteousness. **Your flesh is the sworn enemy of God, and that's where your battle is fought.**

The war rages between your flesh, which you are obviously very close to, and God. Romans 8:7–8 explains that "the mind-set of the flesh is hostile to God because it does not submit itself to God's law, for it is unable to do so. Those who are in the flesh cannot please God." So the sense you have had of a tug of war—the sense that you want one thing and God wants another—even the guilt you feel but want to ignore, all points to those hostilities within you. That's why so many people take a look at God and reject Him. They don't want to attempt the alternative, to reject themselves in favor of God, because self promises them so much. And for many, themselves is all they have, so to reject self in favor of some God they cannot see can be frightening.

But it all changes when you recognize the powerlessness of your "self" to save you. And the danger of giving into yourself and indulging in anything you want. As long as you serve yourself, you put yourself in bondage to the stuff you want to pursue. But when you dare to risk rejecting your flesh with all its complaints, suspicions, and obsessions and instead embrace the life of Christ in you, the freedom you sense will be nothing short of miraculous. When that happens, when you embrace the life of Christ, suddenly the things that used to plague you become unimportant, and the chains start to fall off. So it goes that the people who used to frustrate you, the situations that used to consume you, the fears that used to assault you all fade into the distance as God and His nature takes center stage.

➡ **Hayley's Freedom:** All my life I have been consumed with worry. I worried about everything, from my safety to my success. In college I did five hours of homework a day! I was so worried about getting anything less than an A. When I traveled, I worried about dying in some tragic accident. When I ate, I worried about what the food would do to my health. I am a worrier down to the bone. But when I started to own my faith and allowed Christ to own me, the sting of worry weakened. I was still prone to worry, but whenever it reared its ugly head, I was able to reject it in favor of God. Knowing that He is sovereign and doesn't allow anything to happen that isn't the best for me—even if the best should cause me pain—gave me freedom from the fear that fed my worry and the doubt that enlivened it. Yes, owning my faith in Christ released the chains that held me for most of my life. ⬅

Freedom from fear

Fear is at the root of much of the struggles in your life. Fear offers protection. When you fear fire, you keep yourself from falling into it. So fear serves a purpose, but most fear has to do with where you put your faith. If your faith is in yourself, then fear can easily creep in when you realize you aren't able to protect yourself always. If your faith is in others, the same doubt remains. **When your faith is in anything or anyone else other than God, then fear is your only line of defense against any failure on the part of the creation to save you.** But when you put your trust in God, when you risk all and allow Him to be God, fear is driven out in favor of faith. And while the fear of God is the beginning of all wisdom, it is only so because to fear God is to fear living life without Him, not to fear His punishment or His lack of love and care for you.

When you fear man or any part of the creation, or even a wrathful God, your biggest fear is pain and suffering. And since you cannot ultimately control the pain and suffering you will experience, your fear strengthens as it attempts to protect you. But when you are certain of God's goodness, when you put your life into His hands and say "I trust you," fear loses its power. After all, what is there to fear but God's will? "There is no fear in love; instead, perfect love drives out fear, because fear involves punishment. So the one who fears has not reached perfection in love" (1 John 4:18).

If God is perfect, then so is His will. Therefore, even if pain should hit, you can know that it is perfect and for your ultimate benefit. In this way of thinking, fear loses its foothold since what it promises—protection from a sovereign God—is no longer needed. When you put yourself on God's side, you want Him to win, so there is no need to protect yourself from what He will accomplish in your life.

There is also the misguided fear of not pleasing God. This fear can lead a lot of people to give up even trying, as it did Hayley. You figure He is too hard to please, so why bother; you're going to fail either way. This notion is fear fulfilled. You fear not pleasing Him so you project fear to accomplish what has not yet been accomplished, your complete failure. And as you project that, you allow fear to convince you to give up the trying that led to the fear in the first place. This is a misunderstanding of God's grace. "For God did not appoint us to wrath, but to obtain salvation through our Lord Jesus Christ, who died for us, so that whether we are awake or asleep, we will live together with Him" (1 Thess. 5:9–10).

When you own your faith, you are not under the wrath of God, but have the salvation that God offers to anyone who would take it. Do not try to add to it by thinking you need to do something or be something, but take it as sufficient to cover all your sins—past, present, and future. Remember, **fear has to do with punishment, and Christ took your punishment for you.** He paid the price so you wouldn't have to. So fear is done with—now there is only confidence in Him to protect you and to love you. "The LORD is my rock, my fortress, and my deliverer, my God, my mountain where I seek refuge, my shield and the horn of my salvation, my stronghold" (Ps. 18:2).

➡ "When I am afraid, I will trust in You. In God, whose word I praise, in God I trust; I will not fear. What can man do to me?" (Ps. 56:3–4) ⬅

Freedom from worry

Worry is the power behind a lot of actions and emotions. Worry attempts the same feat as fear, to save and protect you. It offers you something to do to control your world. But worry is ineffective, not doing what it promises. Worry starts in your heart as you consider the fear you've already seen, and it then moves into your body. Ulcers, sickness, stress, fatigue, heart problems, and high blood pressure can all be gifts of the chains of worry. If you worry, then you know what we are talking about. **Worry attempts to protect you from one thing while destroying you with many others.** Fair exchange? We think not.

So how does owning your faith set you free from worry? It's not so different from fear. **Worry is your heart calling God a liar.** It is your feelings feeding your sense of His inadequacy at being God. And it feeds your attempt to take over for those failures. Whether you agree or not, **worry teaches you that God cannot be trusted.**

When you believe God is dangerous and untrustworthy, your only act of protection is worry. But worry isn't protection at all, but bondage. If you are prone to worry, you know of what we speak. But worry really is born in ignorance. It is born in the notion that God isn't capable, and this just isn't true. If God could be tricked, beaten, distracted, or in any way unavailable, then He wouldn't be God. The very nature of God implies His omnipresence, omniscience, and omnipotence. These omnis—or alls—mean that He is never out of the picture, never at a loss of wisdom or knowledge, and never powerless to do anything.

The question you have to ask yourself is, "Can God do something to change my life right now? Is He powerful enough?" If the answer is yes, then you are left with the question, **"Then why isn't He doing something?"** How you answer that will depend on your thoughts on God. According to His Word, He is good without ceasing; He is love; He is merciful, just, all-powerful, and active in your life. So if He isn't doing what you think He should do, it is for a very good reason.

If you were able to see the end from the beginning, yesterday, and tomorrow, then you might see why He does or doesn't do what He does. But you are incapable of such a feat. And so you attempt to cover your weakness with worry. Worry never saved anybody, but it has destroyed many. If you can accept the perfection of God and allow Him to be, well . . . God, then you can let go of your accusations about His ability to be God the way only God can.

To sit on the fence and hedge your bets by not fully committing to your faith is to allow worry to direct your life, and so to become your own little god. But worry isn't out to protect you, so think twice. **Worry is simply your flesh's attempt to remove the risk of faith in favor of accusation.** But if you want to be free from worry, you must stop accusing God and start trusting that no matter what His will, it is perfect and can be trusted. When that is the case, nothing can threaten you, because if everything ultimately comes through the hand of God, it must be good.

Freedom from hopelessness

Hopelessness comes from the idea that success, redemption, and improvement are all impossible. **Hopelessness looks at the world and sees no power so big that it can overcome.** But Christ says, "Take heart; I have overcome the world" (John 16:33 ESV). When the world is against you, Christ is for you. What can they do? When you own your faith, when you own God as your God, you can say, "The LORD is for me; I will not be afraid. What can man do to me?" (Ps. 118:6). The act of ownership puts Him on your side, and it makes you His. When you belong to God, hope is your foundation. It defines your faith, as you can see from reading Hebrews 11:1, "Now faith is the reality of what is hoped for, the proof of what is not seen." Faith and hope are inextricable. You want to be done with hopelessness? You want the freshness and life-giving power of hope? Then you must own your faith—when it is yours, so is hope.

No matter what the state of your life—you are on top of the world or at the bottom of the pit—there is hope for you. There is no pit so deep that God won't lift you up. Even your sin is not a cause for hopelessness. In fact, without faith, your sin is death, and therefore hopeless. But with faith in the life, death, and blood of Jesus, your sin is removed and hope is planted.

If you have failed and your life feels hopeless, you need only one thing: the belief that God is enough and that He will never reject you when you determine to accept the free gift of His grace in the form of His Son Jesus.

In the words of Lamentations 3:21–25:

> Yet I call this to mind, and therefore I have hope:
> Because of the LORD's faithful love we do not

perish, for His mercies never end. They are new every morning; great is Your faithfulness! I say: The LORD is my portion, therefore I will put my hope in Him. The LORD is good to those who wait for Him, to the person who seeks Him.

When you look for Him and wait for Him without making demands or kicking into self-protection mode, He will deliver you. He will save you, maybe not from your situation, but He will save you from yourself and the worry, fear, doubt, and hopelessness that it so easily accepts. **Hope in God isn't determined by what happens to you but by *Who* happens to you.** When you allow God to be God rather than your flesh, then nothing happens to you that is outside of His hand. And in this there is hope for everyone!

Freedom from self

The battle for your freedom is a battle within yourself. It is a battle between the part of you that wants what it wants and the part of you that would reject self in favor of Him. But freedom will never be yours as long as you put self first. This goes against every fiber of your being, but it is nonetheless true. Your self is a cruel taskmaster who demands your comfort, peace, happiness, success, acceptance, and everything that is good. Even if you suffer from self-hate, at the root is self-love. Huh? Well, **self-hate is simply you believing that you deserve better than what you do or who you are.** This sense of pride in your flesh condemns you when you don't achieve the perfection you believe is owed to you, and so you punish yourself, reject yourself, and in other words, hate yourself. But **as long as your "self" is the topic of the conversation, you are in love with yourself.** If you want to be free from the chains of self-hate—if you want to be free from the chains of pride that make demands on your life and lead you to all kinds of bondage-making actions—then you have to turn yourself over to Him.

Faith requires death to self. In Matthew 16:24, Jesus explains this idea when He says, "If anyone wants to come with Me, he must deny himself, take up his cross, and follow Me." This denying of yourself is the heart of freedom. Self leads to bondage, but denying self leads to the life you were designed for, and in this is freedom. As you deny yourself, the power of addiction, fear, emotional turmoil, and lack of self-control all lose their grip.

You were not meant to be your own god, to hold the weight of the world on your shoulders. When you look to yourself for hope, for strength, for answers, then you hold more than you can bear. And this goes for the denying of yourself as well. **Nothing that you do of any**

value spiritually comes from yourself, but all of it comes from the Spirit within you. See, your flesh is not only powerless to save you from hell but to save you from minute-by-minute sin as well. So if you will deny yourself, if you will find self-control, it will only be through the power of the Spirit. But the Spirit will not be your power until you agree with Him and trust Him.

Looking at God from a distance, being an observer, will never save you because it will never give you the power of the Holy Spirit in your life. But when you own your faith, the Spirit owns you and makes His home in you. And then what is left for you is to set your mind on the things of the Spirit, to know His voice by reading His Word, to refuse to listen to the world or obey it, but to allow the Spirit to inform you. In this resting on His Spirit, the power to deny yourself comes to you. But trying to do any of this on your own will only prove a complete and utter failure. As Jesus so directly put it, "The Spirit is the One who gives life. The flesh doesn't help at all" (John 6:63).

Freedom from the fight

For many of us, the presence of broken relationships in our lives is a bondage all its own. But that is not the way of faith. God is a God of reconciliation. He is a God who is, by His very nature, kind and merciful. He doesn't judge you as your sins deserve or withhold good from you on the basis of your failure to be perfect, but gives you all that you need for forgiveness and healing regardless of your merit.

Unfortunately, even though you know God is divine, it can be easy to think of Him in human terms. You've spent your entire life under the authority of other human beings—beings who are not perfect, not always good, and not always kind. Being human, they sin, and when they sin, it can affect you. Their actions can hurt, they can sting, and they can bruise. When living with people, it's easy to get used to rejection, punishment, and meanness. And with each failure of the people in your life to show you grace, acceptance, or kindness, callouses can grow on your heart. Your heart can get hard. When that happens, it becomes natural for your calloused heart to be resistant to trusting in God's grace. Grace isn't something that happens often in the realm of humanity. After all, most of us are very much in love with justice. When we see a mistake, a failure, a sin, we believe something must be done about it in order to keep the balances of justice, well . . . balanced. And so **grace—the act of showing kindness to people who don't deserve it**—and **mercy—the act of not punishing people the way they really deserve**—feels uncomfortable, if not dangerous, to our human nature. When the humans in your life fail to offer you grace and mercy, you can easily then translate that to God, especially if those humans claim to love Him. And you can easily adopt those same practices in your life.

➡ **Michael's Free to Disappoint:** All my life I've been a slave to pleasing people. Hey, I've disappointed a ton of people, but my motivation was always "What will people think?" And as we've already covered, that motivation is all based on self. But something changed when I came to own my faith. I decided that my life and the relationships in it would always be a mess if they were based on pleasing others because, ultimately, I would always run into situations where I couldn't please everyone. Like when a boss would want me for overtime the same night that a girlfriend wanted to go out. Not wanting to disappoint, I'd end up lying to the one who didn't get me. Owning my faith allows me to live to please God; that means making decisions that best amplify Him and being honest about those choices. Freedom! ⬅

As long as you demand justice, you will forever be a slave to justice. But when you own your faith, you become more Christlike. You offer grace to people who don't deserve it, and you show mercy when they deserve punishment. When your faith is founded in what God has done for you—the depth of His forgiveness, the oceans of His grace—what hypocrisy to fail to offer the same to those around you! But we are not judging or condemning you, only waking you up to the chains of justice.

As long as you demand justice, you will live in bondage. But in the freedom of a faith that you own, you no longer attempt to play God by organizing the punishment of those who fail you or fail Him. Do you not think that in His sovereignty He can handle that all on His own? And don't you think that in that same sovereignty He could have made those people act differently than they did (see Rom. 9:11–16)? And if He didn't . . . well, then it was because He saw their action, no matter how bad, as fit for them and so also for you? The Bible is filled with evidence of this. Just look at the instances where God hardens the hearts of people who attempt to control or hurt His children. For example, in Exodus 14:17 God said, "I am going to harden the hearts of the Egyptians so that they will go in after them, and I will receive glory by means of Pharaoh, all his army, and his chariots and horsemen." You cannot know what God uses, who He uses, or for what purpose He uses them; but when you own your faith, you just know He does and so you are freed.

This is the freedom of faith. It is the freedom to stop playing God in your life and in the lives of others; it is the freedom from being scared by, controlled by, or in any way damaged by the actions of others. As long as you are in God's hands, living as His child, you are never a victim. Victim insinuates that your life was unprotected, attacked unfairly, and that you were powerless in your reaction to their crime. But as a believer, you are never unprotected, no matter what they do, never devoid of justice, and never powerless in your reaction. That is because God always protects and is always just—and knowing that, you have the power to react in trust, hope, and love, no matter what sin others might commit.

This doesn't mean you won't sometimes be hurt by people, by bad people, but to point your finger at the people—as if they were ultimately in charge of your pain—is to remove God from the picture. Seeing Him as sovereign gives you the freedom to no longer resent, hate, fear, or worry about those who might hurt you. It gives you the freedom to offer them grace and forgiveness. And in so doing, it allows you to work at reconciliation with those who are at odds with you. As long as you fail to attempt reconciliation—not out of proving your rightness to people, but out of confessing your own sin and letting God deal with theirs—you will never be reconciled. **God wants your reconciliation before He wants your worship.** Jesus explains this in Matthew 5:23–24: "If you are offering your gift on the altar, and there you remember that your brother has something against you, leave your gift there in front of the altar. First go and be reconciled with your brother, and then come and offer your gift."

Reconciliation matters to God. As long as two people remain at odds, as long as there is a sense of resentment, hatred, discord, or disownership, then there is the worship of law over grace. And the entire foundation of your faith isn't the law, but God's grace—His unmerited kindness to you as a sinner. How strange it is to receive so much grace from God but not to offer it to other sinners. It's like the man who took the forgiveness of his debt but wouldn't forgive his debtor. This is perhaps why reconciliation is so important to God; it is His very nature, and so He wants it to be yours as well.

The truth is that reconciliation, or the act of pursuing it, comes natural to the true believer who has owned his or her faith. That's because once you put your faith in Him and you become keenly aware of your sin, you see yourself in the people you formerly rejected. And rather than worrying about self-protection or standing on principle, you stand at the foot of the cross and see the outstretched arms of a savior who is big enough to cover you and the relationships that He wishes to reconcile in your life.

➡ **Saving Faith:** There comes a point in everyone's life when simple belief just isn't enough to win the fight. And that's because belief doesn't save you. When we began the journey of this book with you, we purposefully avoided the discussion of what the "it" of Own It really is. In other words, what exactly defines faith? That is, in part, because if you are reading this book, we assumed your faith was, or is, in progress—not solid, not certain, and not ready for a collegiate definition that would force you to either look at it and give yourself a big fat F or allow yourself to take a C+ as a passing grade. Faith doesn't come from a perfect definition but from a perfect God. As you've been reading this book, hopefully God has been working on you, showing more and more of Himself to you. This is the beginning of true faith.

Faith isn't just the act of believing in God, calling Jesus the Savior, or even saying the sinner's prayer. "You believe that God is one; you do well. The demons also believe—and they shudder" (James 2:19). These words in James make the idea of faith something more than simply belief in God. Saving faith goes beyond simple belief to action—action that trusts God to be sufficient for life. In other words, the "it" that you must own in order to be a child of God is this: faith in Jesus Christ and His death, burial, and resurrection— believing they are sufficient to reconcile your life to God. Theologian B. B. Warfield once said, "The saving power of faith resides thus not in itself, but in the Almighty Savior on whom it rests. . . . It is not, strictly speaking, even faith in Christ that saves, but that Christ saves through faith." True saving faith incorporates repentance from your sin and surrendering your will to pay for your salvation through works or guilt or whatever. Simply resting on the finished work of Christ on the cross saves you from sin and makes you acceptable in God's sight. Saving faith involves both the mind and the will, and both are supernaturally changed by the Holy Spirit. ◀

It Is Finished

Maybe there was a time when you accepted Christ into your heart, when you sought the saving faith you had heard so much about. You heard of salvation from hell, from sin, and from trouble, and you wanted to sign up. So you said the sinner's prayer or something like it. And then life happened. You got busy. You got distracted. You got bored. And the life of faith didn't appeal to you so much. Sure, you want to be saved, you want to be forgiven, but at what cost? And so you doubted your faith, or you accepted it on loan. No matter how you have lived since God first came to you, your faith has not been your own. And that is at the root of all your problems with God. Not Him and His distance, or Him and His rules, but you and your decision to hold onto the things of this world that tantalized you and pulled at you.

Maybe now you are starting to see that what you thought was faith was no such thing. Hopefully God is opening your eyes to see the true saving power of faith. Hopefully He is showing you that the faith that saves is a faith that costs you something, that will change your life, and that will complete you. **When you own your faith, it goes beyond salvation; it frees you.** It frees you to live life with abandon. It frees you from fear of punishment and failure, from worry, fear, and doubt. And as it does, it gives you a new perspective on the people around you. No longer do you attempt to play God in their lives and demand they behave a certain way. Because God is God, you allow Him to establish their steps. And you offer to them all the grace, love, and forgiveness as He has given you.

165

Maybe as you've looked at your life through this lens you have been more and more certain of your failure and of your guilt. Though you might cringe and want to throw your hands up in defeat, you have to know that the deeper you go into faith the more you will be convicted of sin. That's because **the closer you get to God the more you can see your ungodliness.** Not only does His light shine on you revealing your sin, but His glory puts you to shame and drops you to your knees. Miraculously, this is the place your faith takes hold. It isn't in the recognition of your faithfulness or righteousness, but in the sudden awareness of your sinfulness and the deep desire to confess your shortcomings to your perfect God.

So as you close this book, drop to your knees and voice the failure you've proven to be your trademark. **Allow God to be God, and give up playing the part of a stand-in.** Confession is God's allowance for your sin. With it He promises to forgive you and to make you whole. And with it you have access to a faith you've never before known. Whether you are deep in the depths of salvation or about to dip in your toes, this applies to you. There will never come a day when your sin will stop. There will never come a time when you won't need the cleansing power of confession. And there will never be a time when you can give up ownership of your faith to someone else.

Today is the first day of your freedom from self. Today you can say no to the things that used to control you because it was your self that they controlled. Throw up your hands and say, "I am dead; there is nothing left of me to live." As you reject your flesh, you accept the Spirit— and when you do that, your faith changes your life.

Our prayer is that you don't let this day go by without voicing your love to God, without thanking Him for His saving grace and His gift of freedom. We pray that you will find the strength in Him to make your faith your own, and in that, to no longer live in the darkness, fear, and doubt of your double life. May everything about you point to the One who saves, and may you find a faith worth owning—a faith that moves mountains! A faith in a God who never lets go of those whom He loves and who love Him.

About the Authors

Michael and Hayley DiMarco are the prolific and award-winning writers of more than forty books, with two Christian Book of the Year Awards for Youth and dozens of best sellers for both teens and adults, including *The Big Picture, The Fruitful Wife, Die Young, Over It, Mean Girls, God Girl, God Guy, God Girl Bible,* and *God Guy Bible.* Hayley has been a featured speaker at Women of Faith, Precept Women's Conference, Faithlife Women, and MOPS International, while Michael has been a ministry consultant and speaker for some of the largest organizations in the US, including Women of Faith, Teen Mania, MOPS International, Logos Bible Software, and LifeWay Student Ministry. He is currently serving as the Minister for Young Adults and Leadership at their church in Nashville, Tennessee.

GRACE
unplugged

Sometimes, chasing your dreams
leads you right to where you belong.

LIONSGATE AND MARK BURG PRESENT A CORAM DEO STUDIOS IN ASSOCIATION WITH BIRCHWOOD PICTURES PRODUCTION
"GRACE UNPLUGGED" AJ MICHALKA JAMES DENTON KEVIN POLLAK MICHAEL WELCH SHAWNEE SMITH
EMILY SCHWEBEL KELLY ANNA REDMON MUSIC JOHN J. THOMPSON EDITOR JEFF LIPPENCOTT
DARIAN CORLEY PRODUCTION ROBERT HOFFMAN CINEMATOGRAPHER STASH SLIONSKI
EXECUTIVE MARK BURG LARRY MESTEL DANIEL JASON HEFNER ANNE PARDUCCI JASON CONSTANTINE EDA KOWAN
ROSS RICE LARRY FRENZEL CHRISTOPHER M. ZAPPAS ROBERT L. NORTON
PRODUCED BRAD J. SILVERMAN BRANDON RICE JAMES KILLIAN WRITTEN BRAD J. SILVERMAN

LIONSGATE   CORAMDEO   birchwood
[REEL-LIST]   pictures

PG [logos]

graceunplugged.com

IN THEATERS OCTOBER 4